STAR WARS
DAWN OF
REBELLION
THE VISUAL GUIDE

STAR WARS

DAWN OF REBELLION

THE VISUAL GUIDE

WRITTEN BY PABLO HIDALGO
AND EMILY SHKOUKANI

CROSS-SECTION ARTWORK
BY JOHN R. MULLANEY

CONTENTS

INTRODUCTION

The Galactic Republic is no more. It was not toppled in some singular dramatic military strike during the violent Clone Wars; it withstood the onslaught of the Separatist forces. Instead, it was transformed from within, reshaped by the needs of the conflict in the name of security and strength. The Republic emerged from the crucible of warfare as the first Galactic Empire, triumphant in victory.

At first, many people across the galaxy welcome this transformation, for as revered as the Republic was, it proved vulnerable—inadequate to stop the coming change. Imperial leadership, embodied in Emperor Palpatine, uses this overwhelming support to institute sweeping changes. The military swells to unprecedented scale and power. Liberties are curtailed in the name of order. The storied Galactic Senate finds itself increasingly disarmed through procedure and bureaucracy. A generation has grown up knowing only the Empire and celebrates it accordingly.

But there are those who remember the better past, who have vowed to restore the Republic and to rekindle hope. Away from the unblinking eye of Imperial security, they seek out each other, ever growing in number, and work to fan the bright flame of resistance so it can cast the light of new truth across a galaxy….

TIMELINE: COUNTDOWN TO CIVIL WAR

19 BBY

Darth Sidious enacts Order 66, triggering clone troopers to turn on their Jedi leaders.

Supreme Chancellor Palpatine declares himself Emperor, the Jedi traitors, and the Clone Wars over

Ezra Bridger born on Empire Day on Lothal

Former Jedi Ahsoka Tano meets with Senator Bail Organa to discuss sharing rebel intelligence

The victory over the Separatist Alliance was promised to usher in a thousand years of peace, a proclamation met with enthusiasm from a supportive Senate. But from the start, some are wary of the future promised by the emergent Empire. Before the flames of open conflict are fanned into all-out war, many years are marked by embers of resistance that are stamped out by the Empire.

17 BBY

Imperial leader Orson Krennic oversees a test-firing of a prototype Death Star superlaser

The Empire formally activates its stormtrooper program as a replacement for the clone army

Rebel Saw Gerrera hides a regretful Galen Erso and his family from the Empire

Jedi survivors Cal Kestis and Cere Junda destroy a holocron with the names of Force-sensitive children to protect them from the Empire

16 BBY   **14 BBY**

THE MAKING OF A REBEL

Cassian Andor, a fugitive following an altercation with Corpo guards on Morlana One, is offered a means of escape by a mysterious individual, Luthen Rael. Andor accepts the offer, placing himself on the path to become part of a growing rebellion

Cassian Andor serves on Mimban as a cook

While studying at an Imperial academy, Mandalorian prodigy Sabine Wren naively develops a devastating weapon that could be used against her own people

5 BBY   **6 BBY**

Saw Gerrera abandons Jyn Erso in an effort to conceal her whereabouts from the Empire

An audacious heist of Imperial credits from the garrison at Aldhani prompts the Public Order Resentencing Directive

Now a rebel intelligence agent known as Fulcrum, Ahsoka Tano reunites with former clone commander Rex

Leia Organa begins her formal role as a galactic representative of Alderaan in the Imperial Senate

4 BBY   **3 BBY**   **2 BBY**

Ezra Bridger teams up with Hera Syndulla and the rest of the *Ghost*'s crew and begins Jedi training with Kanan

Mon Mothma denounces Palpatine and flees, gathering the loose coalition of rebels into their most coherent alliance yet

Darth Vader undergoes reconstructive surgery after sustaining terrible injuries at the hands of Obi-Wan Kenobi

Bail and Breha Organa adopt young Leia as their daughter on Alderaan

The Bad Batch clones go rogue and former member Crosshair is tasked with tracking them down

An Imperial task force led by Admiral Rampart destroys clone production facilities in Tipoca City on Kamino

Obi-Wan takes infant Luke Skywalker to live with the Lars family on Tatooine

18 BBY

Scientist Galen Erso begins work on Project Celestial Power, a group tasked with building a superweapon

Cassian Andor is arrested for confronting Imperials

The Free Ryloth Movement fails to assassinate Emperor Palpatine and Darth Vader

Mitth'raw'nuruodo, also known as Thrawn, is found by Imperials. He makes a deal with Emperor Palpatine and begins serving the Empire

Saw Gerrera takes in Jyn Erso after Orson Krennic finds her family and forces her father to return to his work on the Death Star

Rebel operator Nightswan comes to the attention of Senior Lieutenant Thrawn

13 BBY

After escaping the White Worms gang, Han Solo becomes an Imperial cadet

Mira and Ephraim Bridger are arrested for broadcasting anti-Imperial messages

12 BBY

THE KIDNAPPING OF PRINCESS LEIA
The Inquisitor known as Third Sister arranges the abduction of Leia Organa to draw Obi-Wan Kenobi out of hiding. Having rescued Leia, Obi-Wan and the young Organa are on the run from Inquisitors and Darth Vader, but are spirited to safety thanks to the Hidden Path. Kenobi and Vader part ways after a devastating duel

Enfys Nest and the Cloud-Riders take possession of coaxium thanks to smugglers Han Solo and Lando Calrissian

Hera Syndulla starts working with former Jedi Kanan Jarrus

11 BBY

7 BBY **9 BBY**

10 BBY

Saw Gerrera and his partisans, including a Lasat, attack an Imperial patrol led by Alexsandr Kallus.

THE BATTLE OF SCARIF
Jyn, Cassian, and a handful of rebels retrieve the plans of the Death Star from Scarif. They are later assisted by the forces of the newly forged Rebellion. Jyn's team manage to transmit the data to the Rebel Alliance fleet in orbit before they are annihilated.

Cassian Andor's contact on the Ring of Kafrene brings word of an Imperial defector, Bodhi Rook, who speaks of an Imperial superweapon

Rebel agents including Ruescott Melshi and K-2SO liberate Jyn Erso from Wobani, recruiting her for a rebel mission

1 BBY

The *Ghost* crew and their allies liberate Lothal from the Imperials, but Ezra and Thrawn disappear into hyperspace

Jyn Erso sees a recording from her father, Galen Erso, wherein he reveals a hidden flaw in the Death Star

Grand Moff Tarkin fires the Death Star, killing many while destroying the Holy City on Jedha and much of the moon

GALAXY MAP

The growing Rebellion does not conform to borders on a map, much to the consternation of the Empire that seeks to stamp it out. Even the most loyal Imperial sectors are not immune to rebel sentiment growing within their borders. The conflict that grows in this era will be an amorphous one, spilling from one sector to another in a messy fashion that the Empire can only hope to contain by adapting its rigid structures.

THE GALAXY

Spiraling from a densely packed core of aging stars and extending out to wispy arms that define its boundaries, the galaxy is the largest framework for understanding civilization. It is so enormous that even an entity as big as the Empire only covers a fraction of its expanse. Traveling via hyperspace helps collapse these vast distances into a governable scale.

GALACTIC FACTIONS

THE GALACTIC EMPIRE

The largest single political entity known in galactic history, the Empire exceeds the vast territories of the Republic in part due to formerly independent sectors conquered in the Clone Wars. It seeks to expand, as all empires do, bringing its firm-handed style of order into the unruly Outer Rim Territories.

THE REBELLION

The Rebellion at its dawn is more an ideal, an objective, than a firmly defined group. The raucous Outer Rim is home to the most fiercely independent worlds daring to push back against Imperial edicts, but even the well-insulated inner systems provide fertile ground for seeds of unrest to grow.

CRIMINAL UNDERWORLD

If the Rebellion is formless, then so too is the criminal underworld. Every civilized world of note in the galaxy is touched, to some degree, by criminal enterprise. United by the pursuit of profit, the underworld welcomes the coming conflict for the opportunities it presents.

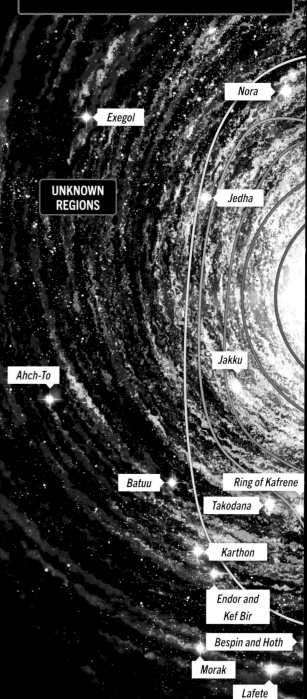

Nora

Exegol

UNKNOWN REGIONS

Jedha

Jakku

Ahch-To

Batuu

Ring of Kafrene

Takodana

Karthon

Endor and Kef Bir

Bespin and Hoth

Morak

Lafete

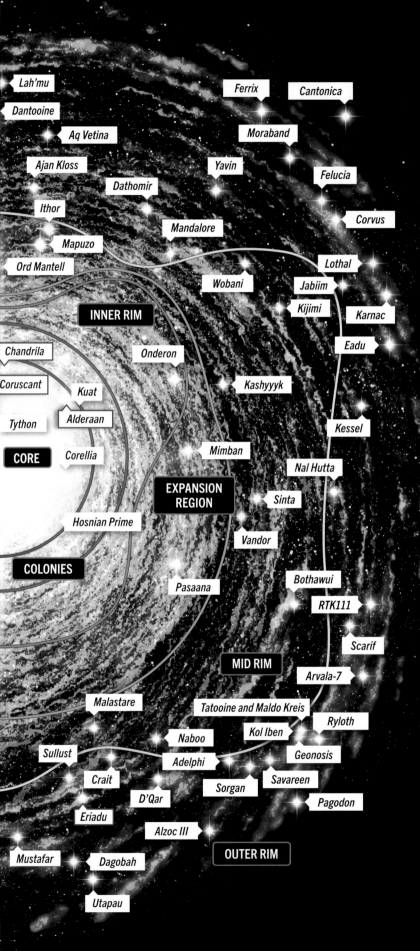

Lah'mu

Dantooine

Aq Vetina

Ajan Kloss

Dathomir

Ithor

Mapuzo

Ord Mantell

Ferrix

Cantonica

Moraband

Yavin

Felucia

Corvus

Mandalore

Lothal

Wobani

Jabiim

Kijimi

Karnac

Eadu

INNER RIM

Chandrila

Onderon

Coruscant

Kuat

Kashyyyk

Tython

Alderaan

Kessel

CORE

Corellia

Mimban

Nal Hutta

EXPANSION REGION

Sinta

Hosnian Prime

Vandor

COLONIES

Pasaana

Bothawui

RTK111

Scarif

MID RIM

Arvala-7

Malastare

Tatooine and Maldo Kreis

Ryloth

Kol Iben

Naboo

Sullust

Adelphi

Geonosis

Crait

Savareen

D'Qar

Sorgan

Pagodon

Eriadu

Alzoc III

Mustafar

Dagobah

OUTER RIM

Utapau

ALDERAAN

A founding world of the Republic, Alderaan still holds political sway even though it may not be as central to galactic governance as it was millennia ago. Its leaders' charisma and clarity keep the planet relevant.

CHANDRILA

A surprisingly pastoral planet amid the urbanized Core Worlds, Chandrila clings to its cultural past to preserve cherished, if antiquated, values. The sweeping changes of Imperial rule prove a greater challenge to weather than the tides of modernity.

CORUSCANT

The single most important world to galactic politics is Coruscant, the layered city planet that has stood at the heart of major historic events for centuries. It is home to the Imperial Senate, the ISB, the Imperial Palace, and the Royal Imperial Academy.

ERIADU

If the Empire had a secondary headquarters in the Outer Rim, Eriadu would be the leading candidate. The capital of the Seswenna sector, Eriadu is the ancestral home of the influential Tarkin family.

CHAPTER 1

ESTABLISHING THE EMPIRE

The Clone Wars were unprecedented, splitting the galaxy apart with warfare on a scale unseen for a thousand years. They were engineered by the Sith to bring an end to the Republic and its valiant protectors, the Jedi Knights, leaving a new regime in its place promising peace and security. The war-weary galaxy welcomed this radical transformation with thunderous applause.

THE DARK SIDE

The secret weakness of the dark side is that it is built on a foundation of fear. The Emperor craves power, so his objective is to conquer all and cocoon himself in such might that he never need be concerned. In open evidence is Palpatine's consolidation of military and political authority. While the Emperor professes a desire for peace and order, the construction of the Empire and the military state complements his spiritual goals.

None know the depths of Sidious' plotting, not even his most loyal attendants.

Some of the Emperor's advisors are scholars, archaeologists, antiquarians, and other founts of occult lore who seek out new discoveries for their dark master. These ministers do not possess Force ability, and in fact, make no claim to understand it. They understand, instead, the historical significance of such finds, and—most importantly—that the Emperor wants them. Should word ever reach the Emperor about supernatural discoveries, rumored Force sensitives, or other mysteries of the dark side, he has a shadowy group to seek out the truth of such claims.

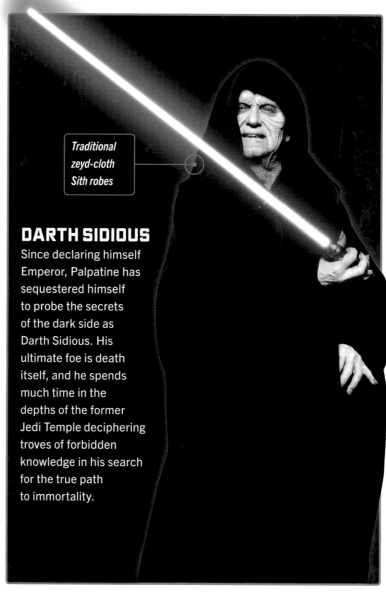

Traditional zeyd-cloth Sith robes

DARTH SIDIOUS

Since declaring himself Emperor, Palpatine has sequestered himself to probe the secrets of the dark side as Darth Sidious. His ultimate foe is death itself, and he spends much time in the depths of the former Jedi Temple deciphering troves of forbidden knowledge in his search for the true path to immortality.

DATA FILE

MANUFACTURER Republic Sienar Systems	
MODEL *Cosinga*-class heavy corvette	
TYPE Custom yacht	
DIMENSIONS Length: 120 m (393 ft 8 in); width: 63.25 m (207 ft 6 in); height: 19.4 m (63 ft 8 in)	
WEAPONS 2 dual turbolasers; 8 heavy blaster cannons; 2 ion cannons; 2 concussion missile launchers (concealed)	
AFFILIATION Emperor Palpatine	

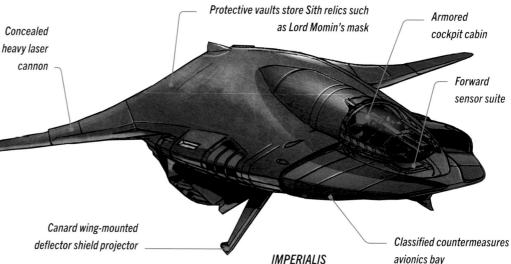

Concealed heavy laser cannon

Protective vaults store Sith relics such as Lord Momin's mask

Armored cockpit cabin

Forward sensor suite

Canard wing-mounted deflector shield projector

IMPERIALIS

Classified countermeasures avionics bay

VERIS HYDAN

Minister Veris Hydan is one of the leading Mortisologists and scholars on ancient and vanished cultures in the Empire. He conducts a thorough study of the Jedi temple ruins on Lothal.

Zeyd-cloth tunic in an ottdefa's cut

THE KNIGHTS OF REN

A group of marauders and mercenaries roaming Wild Space and beyond, the Knights of Ren have some degree of Force ability but not enough for Sidious to consider them a threat. Led by Ren, the Knights' membership has varied over the years.

Momin's paired rapier-like lightsabers

LORD MOMIN

The scholar and artist Lord Momin was an ancient Sith Lord studied by Sidious. Momin was somehow able to use the dark side to imprint an echo of his spirit upon his mask long after his death, allowing a part of him to survive into the reign of the Empire.

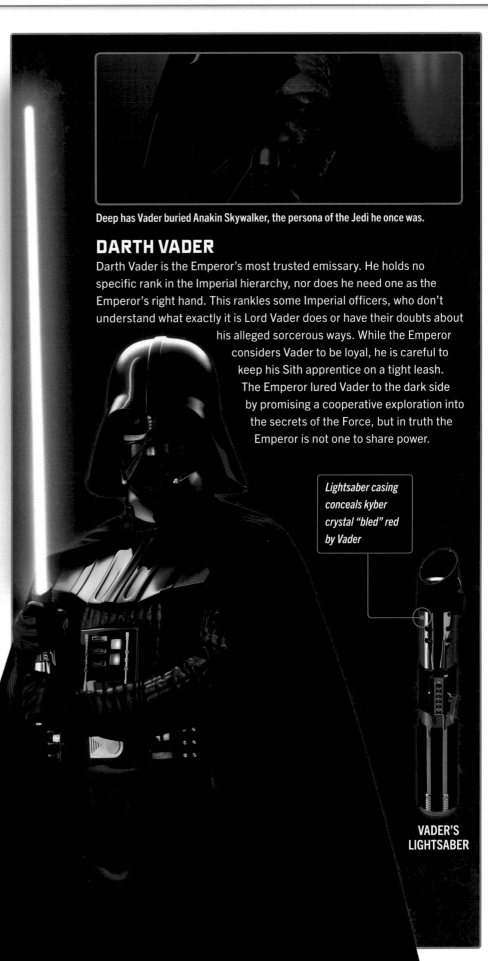

Deep has Vader buried Anakin Skywalker, the persona of the Jedi he once was.

DARTH VADER

Darth Vader is the Emperor's most trusted emissary. He holds no specific rank in the Imperial hierarchy, nor does he need one as the Emperor's right hand. This rankles some Imperial officers, who don't understand what exactly it is Lord Vader does or have their doubts about his alleged sorcerous ways. While the Emperor considers Vader to be loyal, he is careful to keep his Sith apprentice on a tight leash. The Emperor lured Vader to the dark side by promising a cooperative exploration into the secrets of the Force, but in truth the Emperor is not one to share power.

Lightsaber casing conceals kyber crystal "bled" red by Vader

VADER'S LIGHTSABER

IMPERIAL POWER

Governing something as vast as the Empire requires hierarchical, repeated organizational structures of varying scales. Though the Emperor wields considerable power, the Senate is still a very influential voice in galactic politics. The Imperial military is keenly aware of Senate oversight, taking effort to moderate their displays of power while under such scrutiny. Palpatine has a plan to deal with the necessity of the current bureaucracy, but he abides by it for now.

IMPERIAL SENATE

The Imperial Senate superficially resembles the institution that governed during the Republic when corruption festered. Great authority is wielded by Imperial regional governors, and loyalty to the Emperor is closely monitored.

THE EMPEROR

Since his declaration of a New Order, Sheev Palpatine has largely withdrawn from procedural affairs in the Senate, making his rare appearances all the more notable. He has relinquished everyday governance to loyal underlings, a practice that has veiled his office in intrigue.

Active Senate pod floats into debating area

APPRENTICE LEGISLATURE

The next generation of senators enters government through the Apprentice Legislature, a learning institution for the politically inclined. The investiture of a new crop of young representatives is a major event on Coruscant.

Representatives denote disapproval by deactivating their pod's illumination strip

Limited psionic abilities

Traditional Umbaran shadowcloak

ADMINISTRATOR MOORE

An aide to Palpatine during his days as supreme chancellor, Sly Moore is a top-ranking administrator who handles much of the Emperor's public affairs. Her nascent affinity for the Force and interests in dark subjects sees her privy to the other side of Palpatine's power—his secret agenda to accrue unnatural abilities as a Sith Lord.

Speaker's staff adorned with Sistros idol

Chagrian cowl

GRAND VIZIER

The Senate is overseen by Grand Vizier Mas Amedda, a veteran of the chamber with decades of experience. With his booming voice and imposing Chagrian visage, he commands attention and authority. Amedda's permanence is likely due to his effective sycophancy.

Retractable speaker's podium, formerly the supreme chancellor's seat

SHIFTING SENATE

Full Senate sessions are becoming rarer; extended recesses are common, as are abbreviated workdays. Many senators now rely on proxies while they stay in their embassies or on their homeworlds. Each session is either brought to order by the Speaker (the Grand Vizier) or the Oathkeeper, as per ancient tradition.

IMPERIAL MILITARY

The momentum of the Clone Wars, the first full-scale galactic conflict in a millennium, fired up the old forges of military industry. Senate restrictions on such spending dissolved in the name of securing Republic worlds against the Separatist menace. This inertia continued into the emergent Empire, and the militarization has only grown since. Warships and weapons that were once unthinkable a generation earlier pale in comparison to what comes next.

The Imperial military now consists of two primary branches and seven smaller ones. The largest is the Imperial Navy, also called the Imperial Starfleet, comprising the Empire's immense Star Destroyers and swarms of TIE fighters. Next is the Imperial Army, containing the ground troops, stormtroopers, and planetary and atmospheric vehicles that hold and defend surface territory. The Imperial Department of Military Research, Diplomatic Corps, Engineering Corps, Survey and Exploration Corps, Surgical Corps, Military Police, and Imperial Intelligence round out the institution. Imperial Intelligence is intended to work in concert with the civilian Imperial Security Bureau. However, in reality they are often at odds and fiercely compete.

Tarkin scrutinizes reports of aberrant clones while he plans for the future.

GRAND MOFF TARKIN

The scion of an influential family in the Seswenna sector, Wilhuff Tarkin's loyalty to the Emperor and support of his vision has earned him the lofty title of Grand Moff and the governorship of the vast Outer Rim Territories. During a public interview, Tarkin codifies the lessons of Palpatine's regime into a speech that later becomes known as the Tarkin Doctrine. Wilhuff emphasizes the *fear* of force being the guiding principal in keeping order among the worlds of the Empire.

Governor Tarkin shares word with the Imperial chiefs of staff that the Senate has been disbanded, placing regional governors directly in control.

IMPERIAL COMMANDERS

JAYHOLD BEEHAZ
Commandant of the Imperial garrison on Aldhani, Jayhold Beehaz barely tolerates having to interact with the local inhabitants.

TYTAN LATIMER
A lieutenant overseeing gateway security at the Fortress Inquisitorius, he attempts to halt rebel double-agent Tala Durith, but she pulls rank on him.

SODEN PETIGAR
Colonel Soden Petigar is the engineer tasked with developing the next steps and expansion of the Imperial occupation of Aldhani.

MERZIN KEYSAX
A security officer stationed on Ferrix, Lieutenant Merzin Keysax is attached to Dedra Meero's delegation to root out the rebel spy known as Axis.

RANK INSIGNIA

Ranks in the Imperial military are visibly displayed through a color-coded system of squares worn on a rank plaque on an officer's tunic. Inheriting a variant-filled system from the Republic military in the Clone Wars, the Imperial insignia are undergoing a slow transition to a more standardized model. In the current era, single line plaques are the norm, with colored squares indicating service branch, or in some cases, civilian equivalents. Code cylinders worn in shoulder pockets are also indicators of rank or position on occasion.

ARMY OFFICERS

Rank	Insignia
LIEUTENANT	■ ■ ■
CAPTAIN	■ ■ ■ ■
MAJOR	■ ■ ■ ■ ■
COLONEL	■ ■ ■ ■ ■ ■
GENERAL	■ ■ ■ ■ ■ ■ ■

NAVY OFFICERS

Rank	Insignia
LIEUTENANT	■ ■ ■
COMMANDER	■ ■ ■ ■
CAPTAIN	■ ■ ■ ■
COMMODORE	■ ■ ■ ■ ■
ADMIRAL	■ ■ ■ ■ ■ ■

SECURITY OFFICERS

Rank	Insignia
ENSIGN	■
LIEUTENANT	■ ■
CAPTAIN	■ ■ ■
MAJOR	■ ■ ■ ■
COLONEL	■ ■ ■ ■ ■
GENERAL	■ ■ ■ ■ ■ ■

SECURITY TROOPERS
A parallel line of troopers with similar command structure to the Stormtrooper Corps, the black-uniformed security troopers fill positions like outpost guards, prison watch, and civic occupation duty. On Ferrix, these troopers don lightweight army armor to become riot control.

Officer's disc

IMPERIAL OFFICER'S KEPI

IMPERIAL PILOTS

Though Imperial military doctrine undoubtedly favors the immense capital warship, the Imperial starfighter corps are nonetheless renowned. Local flight academies that once produced system-defense pilots, merchant crewers, and exploration service scouts have been co-opted by the Empire to funnel graduates directly into the ever-growing Imperial military.

For many on distant and poor worlds, service as an Imperial fighter pilot represents an escape from boredom or poverty, as well as a chance to make a difference. Some are simply enraptured by the allure of flight and the speed, adrenaline, and challenge found only in the cockpit of a starfighter.

LOCAL AIRBASES

Imperial fighter pilot service is either fleet-launched (supporting the navy) or airbase-launched (air support for the army). Pilot egos have resulted in a fierce rivalry between the two. Space-based pilots are disparaged as "vac-heads," while those serving launch bases, like the one at Alkenzi on Aldhani, are called "groundhogs" by naval crewers.

SKYSTRIKE ACADEMY

After the Clone Wars, the Imperial military command establishes an elite school floating high in the atmosphere of the planet Montross for the top percentile of its pilots. Its purpose is to focus on aerial combat. Grueling curricula create a high rate of cadet washouts, ensuring those who graduate are the best pilots in the galaxy. The flyers call it Skystrike Academy, a name that soon supersedes Montross Academy in Imperial records.

SIMULATED EXERCISE

Rather than risk pilot lives and hardware, early lessons at Skystrike are conducted in simulator pods. Interactive holographic readouts and gravitic projectors accurately recreate space combat.

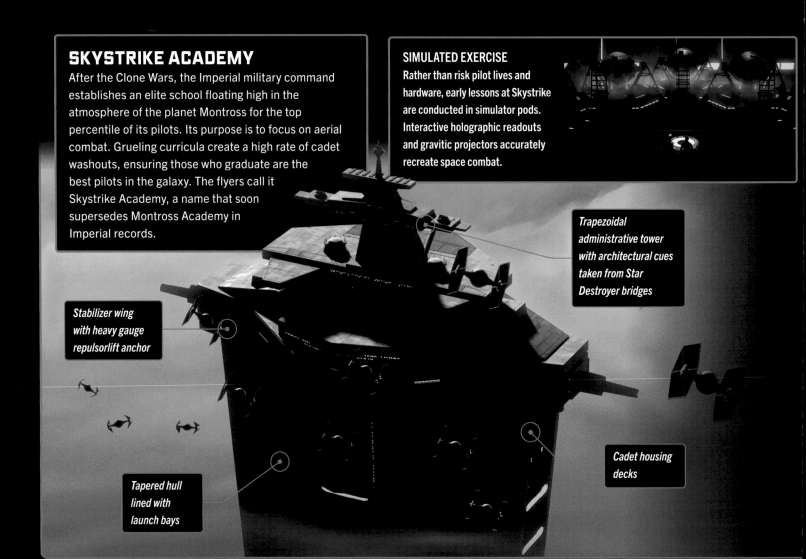

Trapezoidal administrative tower with architectural cues taken from Star Destroyer bridges

Stabilizer wing with heavy gauge repulsorlift anchor

Cadet housing decks

Tapered hull lined with launch bays

GALACTIC SHIPYARDS

CORUSCANT
Clone Wars-era construction and servicing yards are repurposed for the Imperial fleet before the operations move offworld for security reasons.

CORELLIA
Long renowned as a shipbuilding world, Corellia's yards are nationalized for the production of TIE fighters and Star Destroyers.

KUAT
Home of the massive orbital Kuat Drive Yards, Kuat is a major manufacturing concern and political player in the emergent Empire.

CC-24
Sienar Fleet Systems maintains the largely automated CC-24 orbital yards above Castell, a former Separatist planet conquered in the Clone Wars.

VULT SKERRIS

A seasoned and legendary pilot within the Imperial ranks, Vult Skerris teaches at Skystrike to hone the next generation of TIE aces. Thanks to his reputation, Skerris is allowed to fly custom colors and markings on his personal craft. He is a stern and demanding instructor utterly loyal to the Empire.

Skerris' skills draw the attention of Grand Admiral Thrawn, whose cutting-edge tactics rely on precision piloting. Skerris tests Thrawn's prototype TIE defender.

CIENA REE

A native of Jelucan, Ciena Ree has a passion for flight that draws her into the Empire. She attends the Royal Imperial Academy on Coruscant, and though she is a skilled fighter pilot she focuses on officer training within the navy.

WEDGE ANTILLES

A young Corellian pilot with exceptional skills, Wedge Antilles studies at Skystrike Academy despite having no love for the Empire. An opportunity engineered by Sabine Wren lets Wedge and his classmate Hobbie Klivian defect to the Rebellion.

As a rebel, Wedge quickly advances through the starfighter ranks, becoming an expert pilot behind the stick of any Alliance craft.

THANE KYRELL

Also from Jelucan, Thane studies at the Royal Imperial Academy alongside Ciena Ree. They both graduate with honors, with Thane focusing his career on becoming an elite TIE fighter pilot. Despite his admiration for and romantic feelings toward Ciena, Thane fosters growing misgivings about the Empire.

THE RISE OF THE STORMTROOPER

The existence of a Jedi-commissioned clone army ready to counter the growing Separatist movement came as a revelation to the Republic. The soldiers themselves also proved surprising. Conventional wisdom dictated that genetic duplication in laboratory conditions ensured uniformity across the clone troopers, and the Kaminoans lauded themselves on such reliability. But once the clones went into battle and, crucially, were led by the Jedi Knights, their urge for individuality blossomed.

This trend alarmed the secret mastermind of the Clone Wars—Darth Sidious. The secret weapon of the Order 66 command, encoded into each clone's genetic makeup, needed complete, uniform subservience to work. When the time came, the order's execution largely succeeded, but there were a few strong-minded clones who resisted. For the next generation of Imperial soldier, Sidious concludes that unquestioning fealty and subordination can be better achieved through indoctrination, and propaganda, rather than genetics.

Spaceports across the Empire have recruitment officers ready to take in directionless youth with the promise of purposeful service.

Carefully crafted recruitment posters heroically portray stormtroopers as guardians of security and tradition in the Empire.

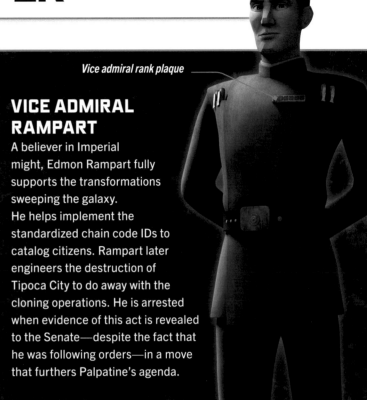

Vice admiral rank plaque

VICE ADMIRAL RAMPART

A believer in Imperial might, Edmon Rampart fully supports the transformations sweeping the galaxy. He helps implement the standardized chain code IDs to catalog citizens. Rampart later engineers the destruction of Tipoca City to do away with the cloning operations. He is arrested when evidence of this act is revealed to the Senate—despite the fact that he was following orders—in a move that furthers Palpatine's agenda.

The aberrations embodied by Clone Force 99 are of great interest to Hemlock.

DOCTOR HEMLOCK

Though the Empire phases out the clone troopers, the Emperor still has an interest in cloning and genetic manipulation. Royce Hemlock, a disgraced Republic scientist, rises to the opportunity in the Advanced Science Division, leading classified experimentation within a medical facility secreted in Mount Tantiss on Wayland.

Imperial science officer's uniform

FALL OF THE CLONE ARMY

END OF THE WAR
The clones listen to Palpatine declare victory and a new future of security in the Galactic Empire.

ELITE SQUAD INTRODUCED
Vice Admiral Rampart introduces the Elite Squad, whose members include the top soldiers from across the galaxy.

PROJECT WAR-MANTLE
War-Mantle is the code name for the creation of barracks, facilities, training programs, and gear for volunteer non-clone troopers.

DESTRUCTION ON KAMINO
Finding no need for the Kaminoan leadership, Rampart leads the bombardment of Tipoca City.

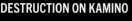

CLONE RIGHTS
Senator Riyo Chuchi questions how the Empire will care for its rapidly aging clone population.

THE EMPEROR'S DECREE
The Emperor declares that all Imperial citizens will have an opportunity to serve in the new era of the stormtrooper.

REPLACEMENTS
At outposts across the Empire, aging clone troopers are quietly replaced by new Imperial stormtrooper recruits.

CROSSHAIR CAPTURED
Dr. Hemlock still sees a future for specialized cloning, and studies the Bad Batch for keys to unlocking genetic potential.

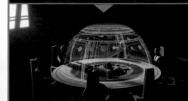

NEXT PHASE OF THE MILITARY
On Eriadu, top Imperial officials determine the future of the military, including the role of the stormtrooper.

Chuchi works closely with Rex and the Bad Batch to save the clones.

SENATOR CHUCHI
A representative from Pantora, Riyo Chuchi loyally served the Republic during the Clone Wars and credits the clone army for the salvation of her world and people. She wants to ensure they are taken care of in the future of the Empire and publicly uncovers a plot that targets the Kamino operation.

Traditional Pantoran crewel-stitch filigree

NAX
Downtrodden on the streets of Daiyu is the clone trooper Nax. He is a veteran of many battles, including Teth, Christophsis, and Umbara, but was removed from the frontlines after extensive injuries. Rapidly declining from age acceleration and neglect, Nax asks passersby for credits.

501st helmet now serves as a credit receptacle

Tattered rags to keep warm

Leg still carries battlefield shrapnel

STORMTROOPERS

The ubiquity of Imperial stormtroopers makes them the face of the Galactic Empire. The Emperor's New Order slowly corrupts what was once a symbol of security in uncertain times—the white armor of the Republic's clone trooper—and turns it into an icon of faceless oppression. Dozens of official and ad-hoc variations of the classic stormtrooper design exist, with more arising as needed to face specific mission parameters or environmental considerations across the galaxy.

> ## "ONLY IMPERIAL STORMTROOPERS ARE SO PRECISE."
> **– OBI-WAN KENOBI**

- BlasTech E-11D rifle
- C-25 fragmentation grenades
- Sensor jammer "screambox"
- Holstered SE-14R light repeating blaster pistol
- Sensor-baffling reflec polymer coating

STANDARD STORMTROOPER

The modern stormtrooper armor is a mix of innovations learned from past versions, but also time-saving measures meant to facilitate mass production within an accelerated buildup. While the armor does boast solid features in terms of sensor interface, environment seal, communications, and modest protection from civilian small arms, it is still cumbersome and vulnerable to heavy blaster fire.

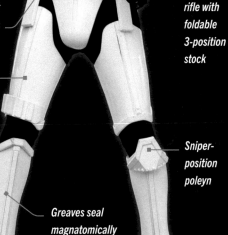

- Helmet dome MFTAS targeting hardware
- Ventilation ports with exchange scrubber
- Plastoid chestplate
- Standard E-11 blaster rifle with foldable 3-position stock
- Stormtrooper utility belt with ammunition cells
- Upper thigh armor
- Sniper-position poleyn
- Greaves seal magnatomically along back seams

DEATH TROOPER

These surgically enhanced elite troopers in stealth-equipped armor are often seen escorting high-ranking officers.

- Air-filtration systems have added dust particulate mesh-screens
- Wide-bore E-11D blaster fire harder to deflect with lightsabers
- Low-light image-intensifying goggle lenses
- DLT-19 heavy blaster rifle
- White armor helps reflect harshest sunlight

PURGE TROOPER

Assigned to the Inquisitorius, purge troopers are elite warriors trained to deal with Jedi. They wield electrified polearms in addition to blasters.

SANDTROOPER

A modest modification in armor and some specialized equipment make a standard stormtrooper more effective in desert environments.

Reflec polymer-coated plastoid

DC-15A clone trooper blaster rifle

ES TROOPER
A pathfinder division for the eventual TK series, the ES are an elite squad of volunteer soldiers in stealth-fitted clone trooper armor.

Helmet repurposed from canceled Phase III clone trooper design

Surplus DC-15A clone trooper blaster rifle

TK TROOPER
These volunteers are the initial replacements for clone troopers. They are the first generation of trooper from Project War-Mantle.

Unit designation color on chestplate

E-22 blaster rifle with reciprocating double barrels

EC-17 hold-out blaster in ankle holster

SHORETROOPER
Coastal defense stormtroopers patrol outposts in waterfront environments while wearing more flexible, lightweight armor.

Helmet with hooded macrobinocular viewplate

Soft fabric midsection for increased mobility

SCOUT TROOPER
With partial armor, Imperial scouts operate lightweight repulsorcraft like the Aratech 74-Z speeder bike.

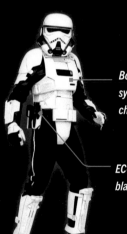

Boosted comms system in chestplate

EC-17 hold-out blaster pistol

PATROL TROOPER
Supplementing local police forces in urban environments, patrol troopers keep order in city streets and thoroughfares.

Synth-fur insulation

Ruggedized E-10R blaster rifle

Utility belt with compact repair and diagnostic gear

Mission-specific magnatomic gription boots

RANGE TROOPER
Range troopers are well-equipped survivalists and wilderness specialists assigned to outposts with harsh weather conditions.

Breath mask filter screen

TANK TROOPER
A specialized Imperial combat driver, the tank trooper wears gear meant to tap into and enhance the drive systems of armored vehicles.

Heat-retaining breather hood

Wind-deflecting kama

SNOWTROOPER
The cold weather assault trooper is the basic infantry stormtrooper fitted with heat-retaining insulated gear for subzero environments.

SPACE TROOPER
Though the standard armor can be sealed against a vacuum, additional gear is needed to operate in space.

Extended air tanks and positioning thrusters

Thermal detonator

Standard armor and bodysuit have hermetic seal

LAVA TROOPER
Volcanic environment stormtroopers have armor bolstered by extensive cooling systems and heat shields. Troops of this kind can be found protecting Fortress Vader on the fiery world of Mustafar.

DELEGATION OF 2,000

As the Clone Wars ground on, leaving profound devastation in the wake of intense fighting, senators expressed their anxieties about the Republic's conduct during the conflict. Of particular concern was Chancellor Palpatine's accrual of new emergency powers with every dramatic turn of the war. Senators were worried that no formal mechanism existed for rolling back these powers as they hinged on emergency conditions that only the chancellor could revoke. Two thousand senators made their dismay known by associating with a petition.

At Cantham House, Bail Organa's Alderaanian embassy offices, alarmed senators met to discuss diminishing political options for preserving democracy.

LIBERTY DIES

The Clone Wars end in a dramatic revelation—the Jedi attempted to take control of the Republic. Palpatine's loyal clone army put down the insurrection, and until the depths of the treachery can be rooted out the Republic is to be reformed. Replacing it is the First Galactic Empire, with sole authority for security falling to the victorious Emperor Sheev Palpatine.

PADMÉ AMIDALA

Like Palpatine, Padmé Amidala hailed from Naboo. She had known him for years, and in her youth mistook his kinship and gentle nature as genuine. She grew to regret her support as his true character became apparent in wartime.

Somber hue reflects wartime tenor

MON MOTHMA

Mon Mothma of Chandrila also harbored suspicions regarding Palpatine's ambitions. Her first priority is finding a diplomatic solution to the war while alleviating suffering. Mothma learned much from Palpatine's ability to project bureaucratic haplessness as a distraction from his true political maneuvering, a method she applies during her time in the Imperial Senate.

TERR TANEEL

Representative of the Senex sector, Terr Taneel is from an aristocratic house waning in power during the Clone Wars. She grows concerned that increased centralized militarization will undermine her sector's autonomy.

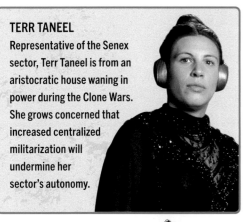

FANG ZAR

Fang Zar's heated rhetoric and dramatic oratory lands him on the earliest ISB watch lists. His home sector, Sern, is home to such rebellious worlds as Ghorman and Albrae-Don.

BANA BREEMU

Bana Breemu represents the Humbarine sector, which saw heavy fighting in the Clone Wars. An intense Separatist orbital bombardment utterly seared the capital world of Humbarine, her home.

CHI EEKWAY PAPANOIDA

Chi Eekway Papanoida is the junior representative of Pantora under Senator Riyo Chuchi. Papanoida acts as Chuchi's trusted deputy for gatherings she cannot attend.

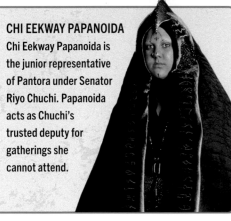

TANNER CADAMAN

Tanner Cadaman of Feenix was one of the most outspoken critics of Palpatine's wartime leadership, venting his dismay in the media. Cadaman is arrested within days of the Empire's formation.

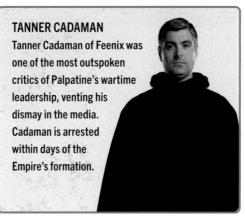

SWEITT CONCORKILL

The Vurk Senator Sweitt Concorkill is a renowned diplomat, having negotiated many truces and deescalated conflicts in his long career. He mistakenly believed he could talk Palpatine into relinquishing his authority.

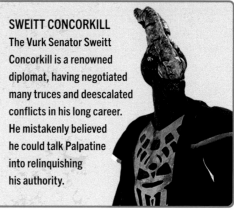

IVOR DRAKE

A friend of Padmé Amidala, Ivor Drake of the Kwymar sector is arrested by the Empire shortly after Amidala's funeral. Despite pressure to name her allies, Drake refuses and perishes in prison.

MALÉ-DEE

Malé-Dee was an interim senator, representing Uyter, who replaced his predecessor, Lexi Dio. He continued her criticism of the executive by signing the petition.

MEENA TILLS

Meena Tills was the Mon Cala representative during the Clone Wars, a tumultuous time for her oceanic homeworld as it faced an internal civil war exacerbated by the Separatists.

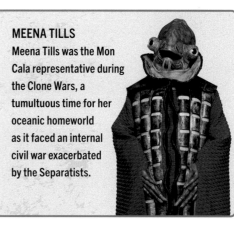

BAIL ORGANA

Alderaan's status as one of the founding worlds of the Galactic Republic affords it great political sway. Bail Organa represents the world and its queen, his wife Breha, in the Senate. Bail steps back some of his criticism to draw Imperial attention away from his family, especially his adopted daughter, Leia.

NEE ALAVAR

Nee Alavar, a Lorrdian, is a good reader of body language and strongly intimates that Palpatine is more than he seems. She vanishes after her arrest by the Empire.

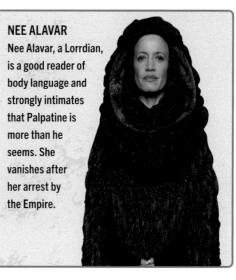

SEEDS OF REBELLION

Though most of the Clone Wars were fought between legions of clone troopers led by Jedi Knights against battle droid armies, there are cases where planets fielded their own local forces. These groups waged war for either the Republic or the Separatists, and some of these combatants factor into the conflict between Empire and Rebellion a generation later. Hard lessons learned in the Clone Wars create veterans who can inform the growing Rebellion as it prepares for a new war.

In this way, the Jedi Knights—though largely vanished—still find a way to shape and inform the spirit of rebellion. The tactics developed by their generals are carefully studied by insurgents, and in some cases these revolutionaries were directly trained or supplied by the Jedi themselves during proxy wars against the Separatists. As the haze of Palpatine's deception clears, it becomes evident that the Jedi were betrayed by the Empire and were not themselves traitors. In recovering the Jedi reputation, the nascent Rebellion embraces the saying "May the Force be with you" as a rallying call.

The Onderonian insurgents originally opposed their unfit king, who had sided with the Separatists.

Steela Gerrera balances Lux Bonteri's caution and Saw Gerrera's volatility.

REBELS ON ONDERON

Jedi Knight Anakin Skywalker devised the plan to arm and train insurgents on Separatists worlds like Onderon, where the Republic had no sanction to wage war due to the planet's history of neutrality prior to its sovereign's decision to join the Separatists. Little did Anakin, an eventual Imperial leader, know he was planting the seeds of the Rebellion. Onderon continues to be a hotbed of insurgency for decades.

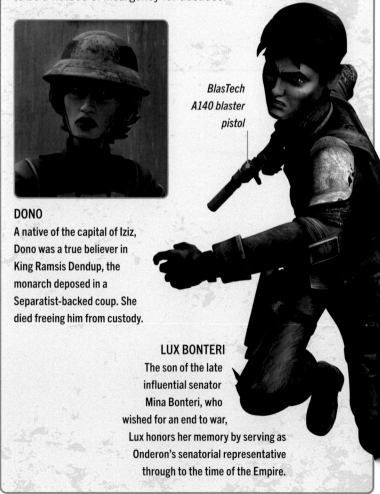

BlasTech A140 blaster pistol

DONO
A native of the capital of Iziz, Dono was a true believer in King Ramsis Dendup, the monarch deposed in a Separatist-backed coup. She died freeing him from custody.

LUX BONTERI
The son of the late influential senator Mina Bonteri, who wished for an end to war, Lux honors her memory by serving as Onderon's senatorial representative through to the time of the Empire.

CLOUD-RIDERS

A notorious swoop gang marauding the Outer Rim, the Cloud-Riders are not thought to be politically motivated. Most would assume them to be typical pirates and thrill-seekers, but it's only through examination of their targets that it's revealed that they predominantly prey on Imperial cargo targets and those affiliated with Crimson Dawn. The Cloud-Riders are in truth an early rebel group.

Unmasked, each Cloud-Rider represents a people wronged or brutalized by their enemy.

ENFYS NEST, LEADER

Electroripper shearing surface

Chromed visor with glare-reducing slit

Vocoder chest box

The Bad Batch relocates Avi Singh and his droid GS-8.

AVI SINGH

A former Republic senator, Avi Singh was an influential politician and outspoken critic of Republic corruption. During the Separatist crisis, his political acumen ensured the Separatist Parliament and capital were established on his planet, Raxus. Defeat in the Clone Wars was a hard, humbling blow for Singh as he truly believes in the cause of independence and sees the threat of an emergent Empire. Singh passionately speaks out against the Empire at a rally and is imprisoned for it. He is later freed by the Bad Batch.

Ames resides in the Governor's Mesa, topped by an ancient bell tower.

Targeting monocle set in survivalist helmet

TAWNI AMES

The Separatist movement had its share of heroes who truly believed in independence. Governor Tawni Ames of the Separatist world Desix refuses to capitulate to the Empire, and takes the incoming Imperial governor hostage. She continues the fight against Imperial occupation until the elite clone trooper Crosshair kills her.

THE BAD BATCH

The Kaminoan cloning process is lauded for its precision, and the fastidious Kaminoans abhor imperfections. Defective clone troopers (DCTs) were dispassionately disposed of and studied closely to pinpoint where the process went awry. During the Battle of Kamino, 99, a DCT assigned janitorial duties, acquitted himself well. Encouraged by the Jedi and clone survivors, this gave the Kaminoans a new vantage point on genetic aberrations.

With this spirit of experimentation comes Clone Force 99, named by its members for their fallen brother's bravery. This unit would consist only of clones with "defective" genomes that have been honed into desirable military attributes. The squad, comprised of Hunter, Wrecker, Crosshair, and Tech, goes on many missions during the war. In time, this team grows and evolves.

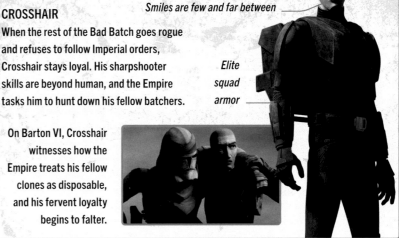

CROSSHAIR

Smiles are few and far between

When the rest of the Bad Batch goes rogue and refuses to follow Imperial orders, Crosshair stays loyal. His sharpshooter skills are beyond human, and the Empire tasks him to hunt down his fellow batchers.

Elite squad armor

On Barton VI, Crosshair witnesses how the Empire treats his fellow clones as disposable, and his fervent loyalty begins to falter.

UNIQUE CLONES

Clone Force 99 takes that inborn inclination toward individuality and magnifies it. These clones accept what was once a pejorative—a bad batch—and wear it as a banner of their uniqueness. Each exhibits biological traits that give them abilities beyond the clone standard, and in some cases even beyond baseline human range. The genetically encoded Order 66 directive fails to manifest in the Bad Batch, and they become fugitives of the Empire.

Solid bone density makes Wrecker hard to knock over

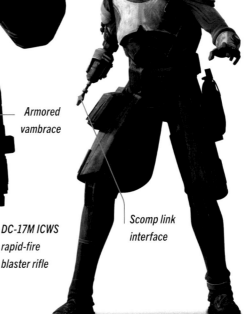

Armored vambrace

DC-17M ICWS rapid-fire blaster rifle

Techno Union custom neural brace cyborg construct

Scomp link interface

Scarf helps confound facial recognition scans

WRECKER

Large in both physique and personality, Wrecker has extraordinary muscle and bone density, granting him superhuman strength. He has a high resistance to injury and is always eager for combat.

ECHO

A former prisoner of war, Echo underwent extensive cybernetic reconstruction following wartime injuries, joining the group at a later stage. Echo can scomp into and infiltrate computer systems with ease.

HUNTER

The Bad Batch's leader, Hunter has incredibly attuned sensory systems. He can naturally sense variations in a planet's magnetic field. Hunter struggles to find a new place for the Batch in a changing galaxy.

NEW ALLIES

FREE RYLOTH MOVEMENT
The Bad Batch aids the Free Ryloth Movement, a group seeking Twi'lek independence, gaining allies in Gobi Glie and young Hera Syndulla.

JEDI SURVIVOR
The clones find a young Jedi survivor of Order 66, the Wookiee youngling Gungi. The Bad Batch delivers him to safety on Kashyyyk.

CLONE UNDERGROUND
Fellow clone Rex contacts the Bad Batch, and with the help of sympathetic Senator Riyo Chuchi they fight for clone rights.

MOKKOTOWN LIBERATION
The Bad Batch frees the indentured miners of Ipsidon, earning the allyship of workers with access to a trove of valuable ipsium.

Data goggles are source of a common nickname: "Goggles"

Magnatomically affixed communications pack

Speeder courier helmet

Zygerrian energy bow

Computer spikes (slicing tools) in ankle holster

TECH
Tech's analytic capabilities, pattern recognition, and abstract reasoning make him the equal of any tactical droid. His mind is constantly puzzle-solving, which leaves him little time to hone interpersonal skills.

OMEGA
A late addition to the Batch, Omega is the youngest member of the team. She shares the baseline genetic template as her "brothers," but it has been altered by Kaminoan scientist Nala Se in as yet unknown ways.

MARAUDER
The personal starship of the Bad Batch, the *Marauder* is a heavily modified *Omicron*-class gunship. The ship is the gang's home as they become fugitives of the Empire, putting down on distant ports or slipping past Imperial patrols using its countermeasure systems or clever piloting tricks. The *Marauder* is briefly stolen on Ipsidon, but the Batch are able to retrieve it.

DATA FILE

MANUFACTURER Cygnus Spaceworks

MODEL *Omicron*-class

TYPE Gunship/shuttle

DIMENSIONS Length: 30.33 m (99 ft 6 in); width: 36.65 m (120 ft 3 in); height: 12.41 m (40 ft 9 in)

WEAPONS 5 wingtip-mounted light laser cannons; 2 fixed heavy laser cannons; 1 rear double laser cannon

AFFILIATION The Bad Batch

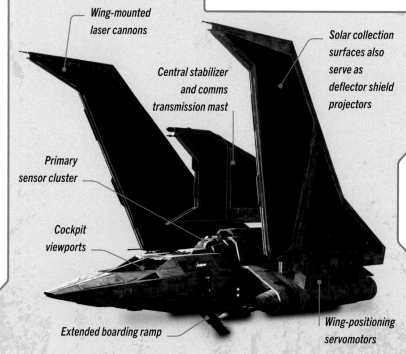

Wing-mounted laser cannons

Solar collection surfaces also serve as deflector shield projectors

Central stabilizer and comms transmission mast

Primary sensor cluster

Cockpit viewports

Extended boarding ramp

Wing-positioning servomotors

CHAPTER 2

THE DARK TIMES

As the Empire's growing authority extends across the galaxy, its enemies seek shelter from the probing eyes of its sinister agents. It becomes a dangerous time for those clinging to the ideals of the Republic and the Jedi. Survival in this era is difficult, but before an armed Rebellion truly takes shape, secretive networks form that are devoted to saving the hunted and building a future.

ALDERAAN

One of the oldest planets in the known galaxy and a founding member of the original Republic, Alderaan sits comfortably among the Core Worlds, and is blessed with verdant forests and snow-capped mountains. Nestled within this natural beauty is the luxurious capital of Aldera, home to the Royal House of Alderaan, who have ruled for hundreds of years. Alderaan is an early sympathizer of the growing Rebellion against the Empire and pays the ultimate price.

ROYAL PALACE

The Royal Palace sits among the other high-rises and boasts panoramic views of Aldera. Its atrium hosts many banquets, ceremonies, and other gatherings, filling the space with an assortment of people. The young Princess Leia Organa often escapes the majestic building to play in the nearby woods.

ALDERAANIAN ARCHITECTURE

In the dense center of Aldera stand some of its oldest and most prominent buildings. Designed long ago by local architect Ar'Ven Vence, these spires were built to emulate the peaks of the Aldera Alps. The sprawling city that developed around them would mimic Vence's work, even long after her time.

Vence spire

Luxury casino and hotel

Native lenall trees

FORESTED WORLD

The lush green forests of Alderaan are made up of conifers and brush and are home to an abundance of wildlife. Runoff water from the snowy mountains keeps the flora and fauna below nourished. Many Alderaanians view the forests as sacred, and some believe they have found enlightenment beneath their canopies.

ALDERA SPACEPORT

Located on the lake bordering Aldera, the city's bustling spaceport welcomes travelers from across the galaxy. A private docking bay is reserved for the Organas and guarded by the Alderaan Guard. As a teenager, Leia launches a relief mission to Wobani, returning to the spaceport with many refugees, who receive a warm welcome.

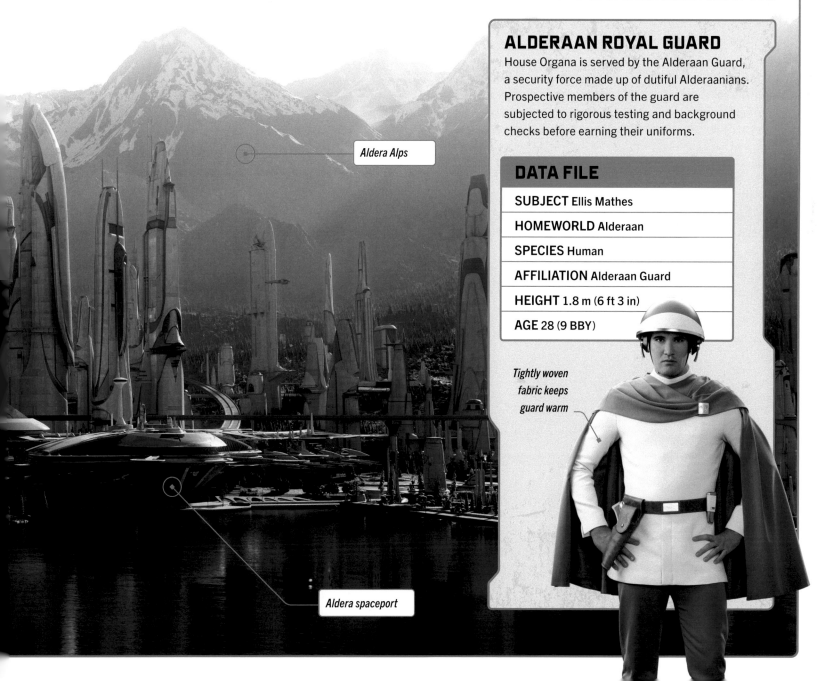

Aldera Alps

Aldera spaceport

ALDERAAN ROYAL GUARD

House Organa is served by the Alderaan Guard, a security force made up of dutiful Alderaanians. Prospective members of the guard are subjected to rigorous testing and background checks before earning their uniforms.

DATA FILE

SUBJECT	Ellis Mathes
HOMEWORLD	Alderaan
SPECIES	Human
AFFILIATION	Alderaan Guard
HEIGHT	1.8 m (6 ft 3 in)
AGE	28 (9 BBY)

Tightly woven fabric keeps guard warm

HOUSE ORGANA

House Organa is one of the oldest families on Alderaan and is a valued member of the Elder Houses: a high-society organization which favors and champions hereditary monarchies. Although the organization held more legitimacy in centuries past, in modern times it serves as more of a social club with little in the way of an agenda. Despite the Elder Houses' decline in relevancy, House Organa remains prominent as the Royal House of Alderaan.

By the reign of the Empire, Alderaan is governed by Queen Breha Organa and represented in the Galactic Senate by her consort, Senator Bail Prestor Organa. The Organas' connection to key individuals during the Clone Wars, including Padmé Amidala, Obi-Wan Kenobi, and Anakin Skywalker, mean they are conscious of significant events the rest of the galaxy is otherwise not privy to. Aware of the elaborate coup staged by then-Supreme Chancellor Palpatine, and that the claims of a Jedi insurgency and an attempt against the chancellor's life are false, the Organas become early conspirators against the Empire.

NIANO ORGANA

Niano Organa is the adolescent son of Duchess Celly Organa and Duke Kayo Organa. At home, Niano can usually be found playing vid-games in his den. In spite of being constantly waited on by droid servants, Niano considers them to be low life forms.

High thread count offers maximum comfort

Large hood to conceal her face

AGIRA

Agira is a loyal handmaiden and friend of Princess Leia. Inspired by the royals of Naboo, Leia asks Agira to pose as her decoy, insisting Breha will find it amusing. The queen is nearly fooled by Agira until she realizes she's holding the hand of an Imroosian and not one of her daughter's.

Princess Leia stands beside her mother and father, who eagerly await the arrival of Breha's sister Celly and her family.

CELLY AND KAYO ORGANA

Queen Breha's sister Celly and her husband Kayo enjoy the lavish parts of high society far more than the drone of politics. Knowing that the throne would pass to any children Breha may have, the duchess and duke moved to Hallyn, Kayo's home city, as Aldera was well represented by the Organa family.

BREHA ORGANA

Like all monarchs of Alderaan, Breha Organa undertook her Day of Demand on her 16th Name Day to prove she was worthy of the crown. She becomes queen when the galaxy is still a democratic republic, and watches firsthand as it transforms into a tyrannical empire. Breha uses her position of power and wealth to aid a growing rebellion.

Traditional braided hairstyle

Breha admires her daughter's latest accessory, a sentimental holster gifted to the young princess by rebel agent Tala Durith. It remains empty, for now.

House Organa seal

Hand-tailored gown

BAIL PRESTOR ORGANA

Born into nobility as Bail Prestor of Alderaan, adventurous Bail fell in love and married Breha Organa as a young man. During the Clone Wars, Bail was the senator of Alderaan where he fought for peace and democracy, befriending many Jedi generals in the process. As a new regime settles into the galaxy, Bail ensures he remains in the Galactic Senate, using his position to subtly impede the Empire at every opportunity.

Rigid collar

Navy blue cloak matches the queen's gown

Leather-bound bracers with House Organa detailing

Bail and Leia link pinky fingers as they come to an agreement about respecting others.

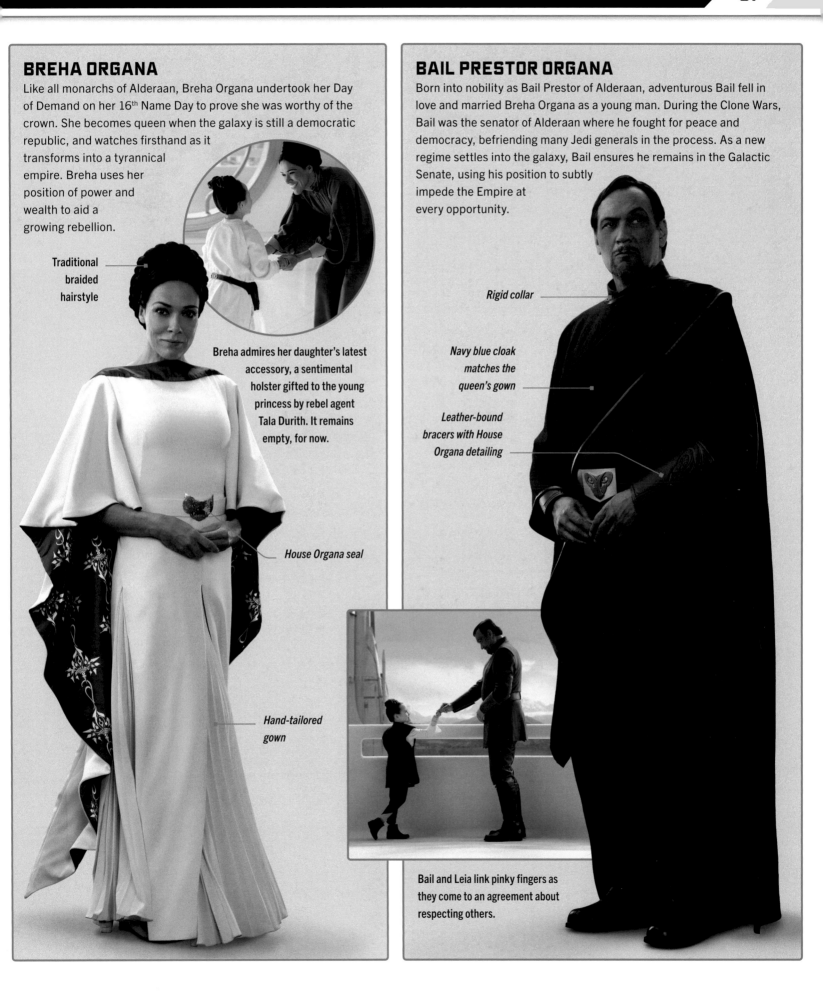

LEIA ORGANA

Born to Senator Padmé Amidala and Jedi Anakin Skywalker, Leia is adopted by Queen Breha and Senator Bail Organa of Alderaan, who promise to love and protect her. Within days of her adoption, Leia is presented at a Name Day Ceremony where she's recognized as the child of Breha and Bail and as the princess of Alderaan. Much like her parents, both biological and adoptive, Leia is a natural leader. She receives lessons on mannerism and etiquette, and is afforded the best education.

A disciplined and protected upbringing only encourages Leia to be more adventurous and curious. The young Leia longs for more than just smiling and waving, often escaping her royal duties to play in the nearby woods. A skilled climber, she enjoys identifying ships coming and going from the treetops.

Leia's true heritage is a mystery to her, but when she encounters Jedi Obi-Wan Kenobi, she feels closer to the truth than ever. Obi-Wan confirms he knew her parents and tells her of the qualities and gifts she received from them.

Obi-Wan Kenobi arrives on Alderaan to see Princess Leia one last time and to return her droid. Leia advises the old Jedi to get some rest.

Leia refuses to give up the people who have helped her, unwilling to give in to the Third Sister's interrogation tactics.

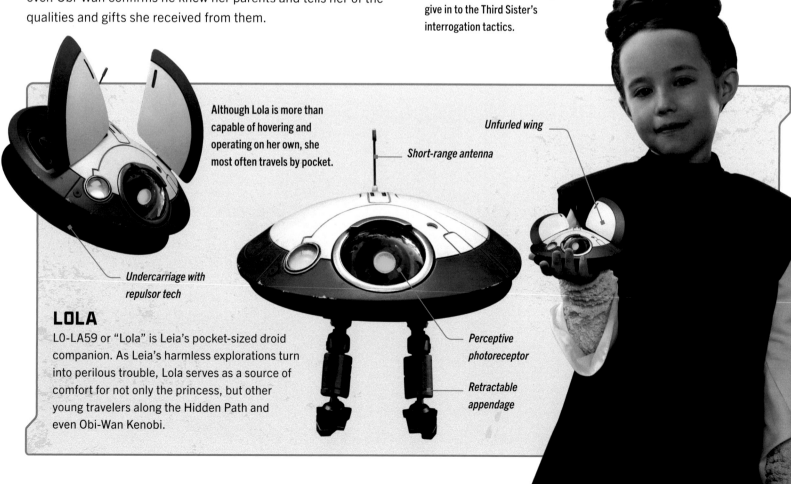

Although Lola is more than capable of hovering and operating on her own, she most often travels by pocket.

Short-range antenna

Unfurled wing

Undercarriage with repulsor tech

Perceptive photoreceptor

Retractable appendage

LOLA

L0-LA59 or "Lola" is Leia's pocket-sized droid companion. As Leia's harmless explorations turn into perilous trouble, Lola serves as a source of comfort for not only the princess, but other young travelers along the Hidden Path and even Obi-Wan Kenobi.

DAIYU DISGUISE

After being rescued by Obi-Wan Kenobi, Leia dons a new belted-tunic and leather gloves in hopes of blending in as they escape her kidnappers and the Inquisitorius. The princess finds a rare sense of freedom in the small act of choosing her clothes, something that's typically decided for her. Part of their cover includes posing as father and daughter, although Leia is hardly convinced that Ben is the proper age.

DATA FILE

SUBJECT	Leia Organa
HOMEWORLD	Alderaan
SPECIES	Human
AFFILIATION	House Organa
HEIGHT	1.22 m (4 ft)
AGE	10 (9 BBY)

Water resistant material

Flared sleeves wick away water from body

Leia uses her size to reach the wires that open the hangar doors on Jabiim.

"IF I'M GOING TO DO THIS, I'M GOING TO WANT TO CHANGE A FEW THINGS."
-LEIA ORGANA

Alderaanian-knit trousers

FINGERLESS GLOVES
Leia enhances her disguise with gloves, and makes a point to feature them in future outfits upon return to Alderaan.

FACT FILE

WOOKIEE DOLL
After an impressionable meeting with a Wookiee, Leia receives a doll resembling the species that she is fond of and keeps it safe in her room.

Handmade artisanal boots

TATOOINE

While most would consider a hot climate, dangerous creatures, and extreme crime to be undesirable qualities, the residents of Tatooine, numbering fewer than a million, find rich opportunities in these less than ideal circumstances. It's thanks to these traits and the planet's astrographic location in the Outer Rim that Tatooine is kept out of galactic politics, although its own public affairs inspire a healthy amount of intrigue.

Hovering cart easily transports stolen salvage

NARI

After spending most of his life in the Jedi Order, Nari has a hard time abandoning his identity in the wake of a new regime. Instead, he tries to balance being a Jedi during the dark times, helping where he can and hiding where he can't. On Tatooine, he crosses paths with former Council member, Obi-Wan Kenobi, but the more experienced Jedi refuses to help Nari.

Shine indicates a well-cared-for hilt

NARI'S LIGHTSABER

TEEKA

The playful Teeka is a master of sales, making house calls to denizens living in some of the most remote locations. When she isn't selling, Teeka scavenges and particularly enjoys the thrill of looting parts and debris at podracing events. Obi-Wan's facial hair is particularly amusing to her.

Audio receiver captures spoken language for translation

ELECTRONIC TRANSLATOR

POINTS OF INTEREST

ANCHORHEAD
Obi-Wan keeps to the fringes of Anchorhead, hoping to cross paths with as few people as possible.

SALOON
A Mos Eisley saloon harbors a fugitive Jedi, drawing the attention of a trio of ruthless Inquisitors.

OBI-WAN'S CAVE
In his exile on Tatooine, Obi-Wan sets up a makeshift home in a cave somewhere beyond Anchorhead.

SPACEPORT
Mos Eisley's spaceport offers a number of transport options, allowing Obi-Wan to easily find a way offworld.

TIBIDON STATION

After a successful hunt, a station is set up around the carcass of a sand whale to harvest its meat, blubber, and anything else that will turn a profit for the whalers. The station will last as long as it takes to pick the bones clean, and then a new operation will crop up, repeating the cycle. Whalers are responsible for hunting and setting up stations, but leave the dirty work of harvesting the whale's contents to lesser-paid individuals.

A skeleton crew guards the station at all times.

HERE BE MONSTERS

The sands of Tatooine are home to many monsters, such as krayt dragons, sarlaccs, and tibidons, but legends claim even bigger beasts dwell in the depths of the dunes. The Tatooine locals have learned which creatures to harvest meat from and which to avoid for fear of certain death.

Hovertrain operated from rear car

Grille keeps engine from overheating

08-Z HOVERTRAIN

DATA FILE

MANUFACTURER Marmoth Factories	
MODEL 08-Z transport	
TYPE Hovertrain	
DIMENSIONS Length: 19.92 m (65 ft 4 in); width: 5.12 m (16 ft 10 in); height: 3.14 m (10 ft 4 in)	
SPEED 90 kph (56 mph)	
WEAPONS None	
AFFILIATION None	

Data sequence is unique to each disc

PUNCH DISC

Handle wrapped in leather made of dewback hide

Shovel groove designed for digging in the sand

Sheathed knife used for butchering

TRENCH SHOVEL

WHALER'S CLEAVER

GROFF DITCHER

OBI-WAN KENOBI

Jedi Master-in-exile Obi-Wan Kenobi has spent the majority of the last several years in solitude on the searing world of Tatooine, watching over the young Luke Skywalker as he grows up on the Lars homestead. Obi-Wan awaits the day when Luke will need tutelage, although the young boy's uncle Owen has other ideas for his future. In the meantime, Obi-Wan practices his own training set for him by Master Yoda.

Other than Yoda's meditations, Obi-Wan has slowly and systematically cut himself off from the Force in order to survive darker times. Now using the pseudonym Ben Kenobi, his cave dwellings are sparsely furnished, and he has little possessions save for a few necessities. To avoid becoming too recognizable, Kenobi works temporary jobs and spends little time in the cities. One of the only constants in Kenobi's life is his pet eopie, Akkani, who he purchases when he first settles on Tatooine.

Obi-Wan confidently locks blades with Darth Vader in a duel of destiny.

Warm hooded cloak to protect identity

JEDI INCOGNITO

After many years in hiding, Obi-Wan surfaces from his Tatooine cave to embark on a dangerous mission across the galaxy. Careful not to draw attention to himself, Obi-Wan wears a long, hooded cloak to conceal his lightsaber and face. The Jedi is keenly aware that he is a high-priority fugitive of the Galactic Empire, and one of the last surviving of his kind. What he doesn't know is how much has changed since his exile, and the horrors that this new Imperial power has in store.

Blue-bladed lightsaber

HARDSHIP AND HOPE

Obi-Wan is still haunted by the horrific events of the Clone Wars. No amount of training from a life dedicated to the Jedi Order can prepare him for how things unfold, and no amount of meditation seems to soothe the recurring nightmares Obi-Wan is plagued with. Despite this, Obi-Wan holds out hope for the future which he knows will be in good hands after spending time with the young Princess Leia.

Weathered hilt from years of use in battle

WEAPON OF A JEDI

The skeletal hilt carried by Kenobi is light in weight yet heavy with the Force. For years, it is laid to rest next to Anakin Skywalker's, preserving all the pain and loss it last witnessed on Mustafar. Kenobi picks up his lightsaber once again, confronting his past in order to light the way for a new future.

TATOOINE TRANSIT

A hovertrain ferrying workers to and from job locations is one of the only offerings provided by employers. Otherwise, workers are responsible for bringing their own water supply and sustenance sticks to keep them going through a taxing shift.

JEDI MACROBINOCULARS

Dark casing absorbs harsh light for optimal viewing

Blaster cartridge front loaded with ionized particles

BR-14 BLASTER

Solar-shielding goggles protect against harsh suns

Lightsaber hilt attached to belt for easy access

Holo technology projects a live or recorded image

IMAGECASTER

> "HAVE YOU EVER BEEN AFRAID OF THE DARK? HOW DOES IT FEEL WHEN YOU TURN ON THE LIGHT?"
>
> – OBI-WAN KENOBI

FACT FILE

Obi-Wan works as a farmhand, a barback, a custodian, and a mechanic among other things in his exile.

DATA FILE

SUBJECT	Obi-Wan Kenobi
HOMEWORLD	Stewjon
SPECIES	Human
AFFILIATION	Jedi Order
HEIGHT	1.79 m (5 ft 10.5 in)
AGE	48 (9 BBY)

THE LARS FAMILY

The small and humble Lars family hail from the Outer Rim world of Tatooine, where they have operated a moisture farm for generations. The family was established by Lef and Gredda, who bore two boys, Edern and Cliegg. Edern suffered an untimely death and was later followed by his parents. As the last Lars, Cliegg departed Tatooine to explore the galaxy. He met his first wife, Aika, and together they had a child named Owen.

Aika passed away when Owen was very young, and Cliegg decided to return to his homeworld with his son. As Owen grew up, he became a diligent farmhand and developed a relationship with Beru Whitesun. In the twilight of the Galactic Republic, the Lars family blended with the Skywalkers after Cliegg married Shmi. Tragedy left Owen and Beru alone on the Lars homestead as the galaxy radically morphed into an Empire. Within days of the new regime's establishment, Owen and Beru become the adoptive parents to their orphaned nephew, Luke Skywalker.

OWEN LARS

Born to Cliegg and Aika Lars somewhere in the Core Worlds, Owen ended up on Tatooine with his father after his mother passed away. Owen is a disciplined person deeply devoted to his small family. Although Owen has many fears about adopting his nephew, Luke Skywalker, he commits to his role as parental figure in the young boy's life, raising him as his own.

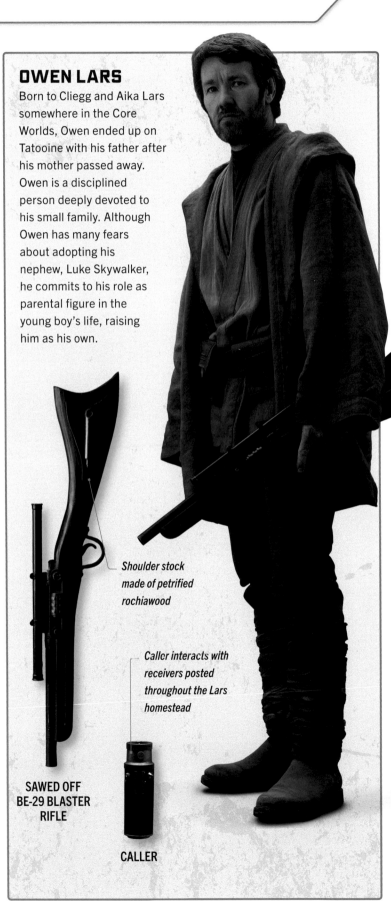

Shoulder stock made of petrified rochiawood

Caller interacts with receivers posted throughout the Lars homestead

SAWED OFF BE-29 BLASTER RIFLE

CALLER

BERU WHITESUN LARS

Born and raised on Tatooine, Beru Whitesun Lars is a multi-generation moisture farmer who marries into the Lars family after falling in love with Owen. Beru is ambitious in everything she does, from agricultural and house chores to homeschooling her nephew. Prior to adopting the young Luke Skywalker, Beru secretly helped deprogram transmitter chips as part of a network that freed enslaved people on Tatooine. She makes the difficult decision to put that work aside after Luke becomes her priority.

Minor carbon scorching on barrel from minimal use

BE-09 BLASTER PISTOL

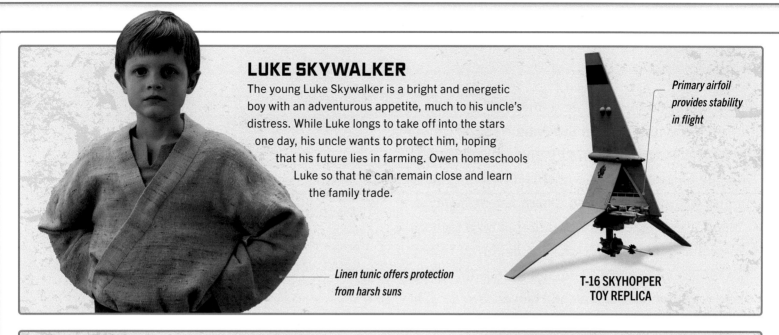

LUKE SKYWALKER

The young Luke Skywalker is a bright and energetic boy with an adventurous appetite, much to his uncle's distress. While Luke longs to take off into the stars one day, his uncle wants to protect him, hoping that his future lies in farming. Owen homeschools Luke so that he can remain close and learn the family trade.

Primary airfoil provides stability in flight

Linen tunic offers protection from harsh suns

T-16 SKYHOPPER TOY REPLICA

DESPERATE DEFENSE

When a revenge-stricken Reva threatens the Larses and their homestead, Beru asserts that she and Owen are enough to protect their own. They prepare Luke for the worst, but not the truth, telling the boy that Tuskens are on the raid again.

CHILDHOOD DREAMS

Luke keeps up with all the latest in Tatooine's podracing, swoop racing, and sky racing culture through comms stations and the local chatter, but has never seen a race in person. He dreams of what it would be like to be at the yoke of a ship.

Chilling bar absorbs moisture from the air

Antenna collects weather data

Empty cisterns indicate a dry season

Storage crate holds farming equipment

THE INQUISITORIUS

The Inquisitorius program is one of many plans in place prior to the fall of the Republic. Darth Sidious correctly determined that following Order 66 he would need powerful and skillful hunters to cull Jedi survivors of the Purge. In a twist of fate, many of these Inquisitors were former Jedi that displayed desirable qualities for the program.

Palpatine kept watch over these vulnerable Jedi during the Clone Wars, ensuring they were spared. Prospective Inquisitors were broken down until they capitulated to the dark side (or resisted until death). Following their subjugation, they were given a number and let loose on the galaxy.

The Inquisitorius program comes to fruition shortly after the dawn of the Empire, and Palpatine gives control of the Inquisitors to his new apprentice, Darth Vader. Second-in-command is the Grand Inquisitor, who leads the order in their day-to-day missions. Infighting is common among the ranks, who have little respect for one another and vie for notoriety.

FOURTH SISTER

Fourth Sister is a no-nonsense Inquisitor. She accompanies the Grand Inquisitor, Third Sister, and Fifth Brother in their hunt for Obi-Wan Kenobi, a fugitive Jedi who Third Sister has lured out in a dangerous ploy. Unlike Third Sister, Fourth Sister abides by the Grand Inquisitor's wishes and only takes action when directed to do so.

Imperial insignia openly associates the Jedi-killing Inquisitors with the Empire

FIFTH BROTHER

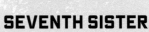

Fifth Brother is defined by his obedience and malice. He often feuds with other Inquisitors, especially those who step out of line. In the past, he has even gotten others killed for their insubordination. Fifth Brother claims he's next in line to become Grand Inquisitor, although there's no guarantee among their ranks.

Standard tactical belt equipped with comlink and lightsaber clip

Second Sister only removes her helmet to reveal her identity when it is advantageous to her.

SECOND SISTER

A Padawan at the time of Order 66, Trilla Suduri is betrayed by her own master, who succumbs to Imperial torture and gives up her apprentice's location. Trilla is then subjected to torture herself, and after submitting to the dark side she becomes part of the Inquisitorius as Second Sister.

SEVENTH SISTER

The ruthless Seventh Sister has served the Inquisitorius for nearly as long as the Empire's existence. More than a decade after the formation of the Inquisitorius program, Seventh Sister and Fifth Brother hunt down rebel Jedi fugitives Kanan Jarrus and Ezra Bridger following the death of the Grand Inquisitor.

Intricate carvings on the lightsaber hilt

The true identity of Eighth Brother is concealed behind his mask.

EIGHTH BROTHER

The Eighth Brother is incredibly acrobatic, a trait of his species, Terrelian Jango Jumper. Like all Inquisitors, he wields a double-bladed lightsaber, which has been slightly modified to his liking with retractable buzzsaw blades. The Eighth Brother shows a fierce dedication to Darth Sidious.

NINTH SISTER

Masana Tide becomes the Ninth Sister in the early days of the Empire, training under both the Grand Inquisitor and Darth Vader. She has gone on many missions with the Dark Lord, including to Cabarria and Dac City. Ninth Sister meets her fate at the hands of Cal Kestis on Coruscant.

TENTH BROTHER

Tenth Brother was once a Jedi Master called Prosset Dibs, who served alongside the likes of Mace Windu and Kit Fisto. Early on in the Clone Wars, Dibs determined that the Republic was no better than the Separatists. When the Empire forms, he believes its rhetoric and pledges himself to the Inquisitorius when the time comes.

THIRTEENTH SISTER

The Thirteenth Sister does not know where she comes from and has never seen another person like her. Raised a Jedi, Akaris was apprenticed to Jedi Master Sember Vey, and the pair were members of the Jedi strike force tasked with rescuing Obi-Wan Kenobi, Anakin Skywalker, and Padmé Amidala from the Separatists on Geonosis.

THE GRAND INQUISITOR

Once a Jedi Temple Guard, the Pau'an served the Order dutifully for many years. Curious about the vast knowledge the Jedi held, he sought to dig through the Order's troves of secured datafiles and holobooks, only to be routinely denied by superior Jedi. This ultimately led to the Pau'an's descent to the dark side upon the execution of Order 66, resulting in his transformation into the Grand Inquisitor. His knowledge of the Jedi is a powerful asset in his quest to hunt them down.

On the hunt for a fugitive Jedi, the Grand Inquisitor arrives on Tatooine flanked by Third Sister and Fifth Brother.

Reinforced pauldron protects against deft attacks

Custom fit tasset

GRAND INQUISITOR BADGE

Whoever holds the title of Grand Inquisitor wears this badge on their armor and a figurative target on their back.

REVA

Reva was only 12 years old on the night of the Great Jedi Purge, when she saw her masters and peers slaughtered by the very clones that were supposed to serve them. But the greatest betrayal came with the arrival of Anakin Skywalker, who Reva thought was there to save them, and his subsequent massacre of her clanmates. Although she, too, was impaled by Skywalker's saber, Reva survived her injuries and the Purge.

Unlike most other Inquisitors, Reva was not scouted by Palpatine to join the Inquisitorius program. Instead, the vengeful Reva later succumbs to the dark side on her own terms and plots to join herself. As the Third Sister, Reva spends years hunting fugitive Jedi in an effort to hone her skills and pursue her true nemesis, Darth Vader, who she knows is Anakin beneath the mask.

REVA'S WEAPONS

Reva is proficient with many weapons, but like all Inquisitors she wields a double-bladed spinning lightsaber that she's slightly customized to complement her fighting style. She also carries throwing knives, which she uses when her saber isn't available.

REVA'S LIGHTSABER

The kybers powering the Third Sister's lightsaber once belonged to Jedi lost to the Purge and were "bled" by Reva herself.

Reva keeps the edge sharp

THROWING KNIVES

Reva forges her own knives, mistrustful of Imperials or droids to take the care and skill she believes is required to craft the weapons.

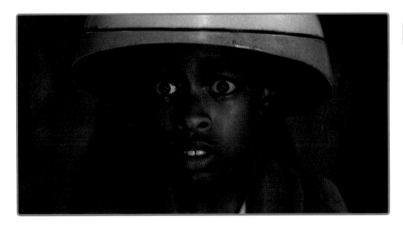

JEDI SURVIVOR

The young and confused Reva bears witness to the horrific slaughter of her clanmates at the hands of Anakin. As a result of this traumatic experience, Reva faces severe survivor's guilt that leads her down a dark path to revenge.

JAR'KAI COMBATANT

Naturally ambidextrous, Reva has been drawn to the art of Jar'Kai since she was a young Jedi Initiate. Under the tutelage of the Grand Inquisitor, Reva perfects her Jar'Kai skills and customizes her Inquisitor hilt to split in half. Some of the greatest masters of both light and dark were trained in this combat style.

White-hot blade capable of cauterizing flesh

Steel-toed combat boots

Echoing a time when Jedi were served by clone troopers, in the Imperial era Inquisitors are flanked by stormtroopers.

DATA FILE

SUBJECT	Reva
HOMEWORLD	Unknown
SPECIES	Human
AFFILIATION	Jedi Order (formerly); Inquisitorius
HEIGHT	1.7 m (5 ft 7 in)
AGE	22 (9 BBY)

Plastoid armor protects against blaster fire

Heat-resistant glove protects hands in duels

"WHERE WERE YOU WHEN HE WAS KILLING MY FRIENDS?

– REVA

Lightsaber is roughly 2.35 m when both blades are ignited

After the apparent death of the Grand Inquisitor, the Third Sister is promoted to take his place. She then speaks directly with Darth Vader regarding the hunt for Obi-Wan Kenobi.

Blades rotate at exponential speeds on outer ring

FACT FILE

FAR-FLUNG MISSIONS
In her time as an Inquisitor, the Third Sister has hunted surviving Jedi and Force sensitives throughout the galaxy, including on Pantora, Valo, Cerea, Boz Pity, and Alsakan.

INQUISITOR ARMOR
The Third Sister's armor has been tailored to her liking, with lightweight sheathing and flexible leggings that serve to both protect her and complement her combat style. Concealed behind her leather plackart are cybernetic replacements she received sometime after being impaled during the Purge. A black cape to intimidate her prey completes the look.

FORTRESS INQUISITORIUS

The Inquisitors originally operate from The Works on Coruscant, but are relocated after causing too much trouble on the capital world. They then set up in a leaky underwater structure on the moon Nur, which orbits Vader's planet, Mustafar. Survivors of the Great Jedi Purge are taken to this foreboding base to be tortured, entombed, or turned into Inquisitors. The intimidating tower, looming over the oceans of the moon, is constructed later to complement Vader's Castle on the nearby volcanic world.

Black stone collected from Mustafar

Exterior hangar allows fighter squadron easy deployment

NUR

The moon of Nur is covered in sodium-rich water and no natural land masses are charted. Unlike Mustafar, upon which Fortress Vader is built, it appears to sustain no sentient life, with Fortress Inquisitorius its only known structure.

DATA FILE

REGION	Outer Rim Territories
DIAMETER	4,000 km (2,485 miles)
TERRAIN	Ocean-covered
POPULATION	No indigenous population

DELIBERATIONS

Third Sister, Fourth Sister, and Fifth Brother strategize with key Imperial personnel after Obi-Wan Kenobi successfully breaches the fortress to rescue Princess Leia. The facility is put on high alert and locked down.

OFFICE OF THE INQUISITORIUS
This stark room contains only chairs and a strategy table. The head seat is reserved for the Grand Inquisitor.

TYTAN LATIMER

CENTRAL HANGAR BAY

Ships arriving and departing from Fortress Inquisitorius are subjected to thorough scans, ensuring the security of the facility. The hangar bay is fully stocked with its own fighter squadron and is often busy with personnel servicing the ships and docks. It is the only access point to the fortress above the water.

SECURITY SCANNER
Manufactured by DeTECHt, the security scanners at Fortress Inquisitorius scan for weapons, bombs, hazardous materials, and other possible threats.

JEDI EXPOSED
Velerie Tide hid her identity following the Great Jedi Purge, blending in with the locals on Athio III, but was captured after being revealed as a Force user.

JEDI TOMB

In the depths of the fortress is a tomb filled with bodies of captured Jedi, preserved in amber. Youngling Faris still wears his training helmet from the night the Temple was attacked, and Jedi Tera Sinube, a master since the High Republic, appears to have never let his robes go either.

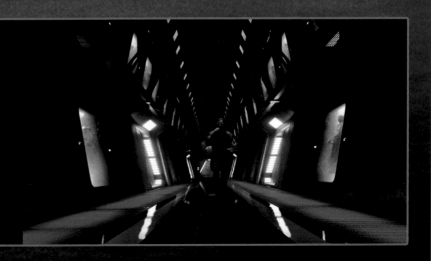

HIDDEN PATH

In the wake of Order 66, surviving Jedi often find themselves alone, leery, and living according to the last order they were given—stay away from the Jedi Temple. It's the Hidden Path's mission to find these Jedi before the Empire does, and give them a second chance at life through a carefully plotted underground network. Through this route, Jedi relinquish their robes, lightsabers, and names in order to survive. The final destination of the Path is an undisclosed safe location.

Although the Hidden Path is born in reaction to the Great Jedi Purge and the creation of the Empire, some of its operation echoes a long-ago society that once sought to reform Jedi and Force users into "regular" citizens by encouraging them to abandon their practices. However, the Hidden Path forms so quickly that its exact origins are hard to trace. Following the infiltration of safe houses on Mapuzo and Jabiim, Jedi survivor Cal Kestis and Nightsister Merrin prepare the recently rediscovered planet Tanalorr for the Hidden Path.

HAJA ESTREE

Haja Estree is a master of illusions, fronting as a Jedi and preying on vulnerable Force sensitives for credits. Although Haja cons these people, their safety is assured as he connects them with the Hidden Path. After meeting a real Jedi Knight, Haja gains a newfound respect for the people he used to swindle.

Conduit connects remote to power bank

MODIFIED REMOTE DOOR OPENER

TALA DURITH

Tala Durith joins the Empire early on in its formation, initially believing in its order, but quickly becomes disillusioned after a mission requires her to kill innocent people for showing signs of Force sensitivity. This situation leads Tala to discover the Hidden Path, where she finds purpose in helping the very people the Imperials seek to harm. Tala keeps her rank within the Empire, using her position to secretly aid the Path.

Muzzle brake disperses energy to counteract recoil

WE-11 BLASTER PISTOL

Tala Durith uses her Imperial cover to help rescue Princess Leia from Fortress Inquisitorius.

MAPUZO SAFE HOUSE

The Hidden Path's Mapuzo safe house is just one in a web of locations where Force sensitives in the galaxy can find refuge and passage to new beginnings. The Mapuzo facility is deemed compromised after the Third Sister discovers its existence.

KAWLAN ROKEN

Kawlan Roken once fell in love with and married a Force-sensitive woman who was tragically murdered by the Inquisitorius. After the loss of his wife, Roken joins the Hidden Path, committing to a life rebelling against the Empire.

— *Authentic Wookiee-carved bowcaster*

NED-B

As is standard for most loadlifters, NED-B cannot speak. Despite this, the droid is more than capable of making its intentions known through deliberate actions.

Barrel coated in heat-resistant alloy

MODIFIED E-5 BLASTER PISTOL

Metal mallet used for securing crates

JABIIM

The silt-covered world of Jabiim is mostly known for its mining operations and as a way station for travelers with more attractive destinations. The Hidden Path has a safe house on the planet, serving as the penultimate destination for the Force sensitives they aid. The safe house is discovered by the Inquisitorius in the midst of the Imperial era, and is abandoned.

Wide entry ramp designed to withstand heavy cargo

Equipped with both sublight engines and a hyperdrive

Cockpit controls prepped for takeoff

Modified T-47 airspeeder has extra cockpit capacity

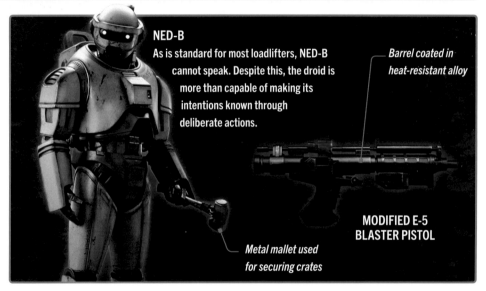

CHAPTER 3

WORLDS OF UNREST

A small number of systems rebel at the new outrages perpetrated by the Empire as their freedoms are ground beneath the boot of Imperial oppression. Reprisals can be swift and, away from Senate attention, brutal, but the embers of resistance continue to burn. From the beginning, these worlds are vastly outnumbered by the systems held in thrall by the Emperor.

RYLOTH

Homeworld of the Twi'leks, Ryloth has a mineral-rich surface that conceals troves of medicinal ryll spice (which can be turned far too easily into a commercial narcotic) and starship-grade doonium ore. Both the world and its people have been frequently exploited by offworlders, and many Twi'leks have been kidnapped and enslaved throughout their tumultuous history. Despite such hardships its people endure, with many desiring freedom and independence. Twi'leks are understandably skeptical of outsiders, preferring isolation—even in the fight against the Empire.

> **"WE'RE FIGHTING FIRST FOR A FREE RYLOTH, NOT TO TOPPLE THE EMPIRE."**
> – CHAM SYNDULLA

DATA FILE

REGION	Outer Rim Territories
SECTOR	Gaulus sector
SYSTEM	Ryloth
DIAMETER	10,600 km (6,587 miles)
TERRAIN	Forest, plains, mountains, deserts
MOONS	5
POPULATION	1.5 billion

Lonely Five rock formation, Kala'uun starport

LUNAR RENDEZVOUS
The shadowed moons of Ryloth, especially its habitable Third Moon, are ideal settings for discreet meetings of would-be insurrectionists of the Free Ryloth Movement.

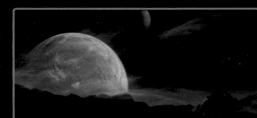

The Cazne Expanse

TWI'LEKS

The Twi'leks are the humanoid natives of Ryloth, known for the long, fleshy protuberances—lekku—growing from their skulls. Trade and unrest spread their populations far from Ryloth, and they can be encountered across the galaxy. Senator Orn Free Taa represents Ryloth in the Galactic Senate, a comfortable position he has occupied for decades.

RYLOTH LOCATIONS

LESSU CITY
The planet's capital, Lessu City, is carved into an enormous spire of rock and is joined to the surrounding lands by a singular plasma bridge.

THE CAPITAL BUILDING
The 700-year-old capital building in the Octagon district is the base of operations for the Ryloth Head Clan, a five-member council.

DOONIUM MINE
Not far from Tann Province is a newly opened Imperial doonium mine which promises new jobs and prosperity for the Twi'leks.

THE SECRET BASE
The burgeoning Free Ryloth Movement uses secret bases and tunnels mapped during the Clone Wars for meetings with allies.

From the protection of his estate, Cham Syndulla stays in touch with allies who inform him of suspicious Imperial activity. Weary of war, he must once again don the mantle of freedom fighter.

ELENI SYNDULLA'S KALIKORI

TWI'LEK FAMILIES
Lineage is very important to Twi'leks, given how often their own family histories are disrupted by strife. Many forms of local artwork emphasize the recording of family events and connections in different types of media meant to ensure permanence.

SYNDULLA FAMILY GLASS MOSAIC PORTRAIT

Crashed Republic Y-wing serves as Clone Wars memorial

Multistory balconies, with family quarters at top and mezzanine guest quarters

Large courtyard for holding outdoor gatherings

Stone wall to keep out wild gutkurrs

SYNDULLA ESTATE
A mountainside property built in the Tann Province, the Syndulla Estate was intended to be a place where Cham could retire, spend time with his family, and write his memoirs about the liberation of Ryloth. Guiding the planet through peacetime required more work than Cham expected, and his home became a remote office for his political work in Lessu.

RYLOTH RESISTANCE

Ryloth has been repeatedly plundered throughout galactic history. The Twi'leks' folkscrolls and sculptures chronicle heroes across the ages that have battled oppressors. The tradition of resistance found a new hero in Cham Syndulla during the Clone Wars, as he led bands of rebels to fight back against Separatist invaders. A fleeting peace reigns, and for a time Syndulla fondly imagines that he can concentrate on raising a family rather than toppling an Empire.

But the respite is short-lived, and the Empire invades the planet. An Imperial doonium mine turns Ryloth into a vital part of the regime's military supply chain, so the fight continues in this new era with Cham Syndulla once again taking up arms.

YENDOR BRETHEN

Yendor joins the Rebellion after word of Hera Syndulla's exploits as part of Phoenix cell spreads through his home city of Rhovari. He hones his piloting skills, learned from dusting whiptree groves, into service as a Y-wing pilot at Tierfon and later as a snowspeeder pilot at Echo Base on Hoth.

BLURRGS

Blurrgs are tough-skinned, dim-witted, omnivorous reptiles found on scattered worlds of the Outer Rim, including Arvala-7, Miv'rah, and Ryloth—where they dwell in the Cazne flatlands. Their high-domed, thick skulls and low centers of gravity make them adept at ramming attacks. Agitated blurrgs may charge and trample indiscriminately.

Gaping mouth helps regulate internal body heat

GOBI GLIE

Burly yet soft-spoken, Gobi Glie has the heart of both a warrior and a troubadour. He has written numerous ballads celebrating Cham Syndulla's rise as a folk hero, having served alongside him in the fight for liberation for decades. Their friendship cools when Cham decides to step away from the fight, but returns even stronger when his ally picks up his blaster once more.

Gobi helps raise Numa, an orphan of the Clone Wars, training her to be an effective resistance fighter against the Empire.

DATA FILE

SPECIES Blurrg

HOMEWORLD
Various in the Outer Rim

DIMENSIONS Height (at withers):
1.98 m (6 ft 6 in); length: 4 m (13 ft 1 in)

LIFESPAN 35-40 standard years,
depending on breed

Blurrgs are capable of surprising speeds over flat surfaces.

The Syndullas consider Gobi to be extended family, with Hera regarding him as an uncle.

Tann Province ancestral markings

Dense nerve endings make lekku very sensitive to touch

ELENI

During the Clone Wars, Eleni helped keep the noncombatants among the Ryloth resistance safe, including young Hera. The tragedies of the war and the fragility of safety are still vivid memories, so the Syndullas turn away from the conflict, eager to believe the peace promised by the Galactic Empire.

CHAM

Cham Syndulla rose from political firebrand to a legendary war hero called the Hammer of Ryloth. His liberation of Lessu from Separatist occupation becomes required study in military academies abroad. Cham feared that accepting Republic help in the Clone Wars would be trading one occupier for another. The Empire proves his misgivings to be well-founded.

Mycofiber fabric spun from cavern fungus

Studied stance of nobility

"MY DREAM WAS FOR A FREE RYLOTH. FOR OUR PEOPLE TO HAPPILY LIVE IN A WORLD AT PEACE."

- CHAM SYNDULLA

HERA

Hera grew up in shelters during the Clone Wars, peering out from cover to see the Republic pilots soar above in their starfighters. When Eleni dies in the fight against the Galactic Empire, driving a wedge between Hera and Cham, Hera leaves Ryloth to pursue her dream of becoming a pilot.

FERRIX

Ferrix has been a key location for the salvage trade for eight centuries due to its convenient location at the intersection of several bustling hyperspace lanes. Unlike the junk worlds of Bracca, Ronyards, and Lotho Minor, where the debris of galactic civilization lies largely inactive, Ferrix has a vibrant community dedicated to refurbishing castaway technology, and its society has evolved around this steady trade.

Communities expand from the salyards: storefronts where wares are bid for, brokered, stripped, repaired, restored, and cataloged for customers. From this economy of recycling comes the infrastructure necessary to turn empty fields into farmlands and austere flatlands into warm homes. Though dependent on offworld buyers, Ferrix has gained a strong sense of cultural identity from the effort involved in transforming discards into desirables, with the daily work cycle marked by a resounding gong of salvaged Mandalorian steel—beskar—in the city square.

HOTEL RIX
The Hotel Rix has reliable—if simple—amenities for offworld traders. The Imperial occupiers set up a base in this building, turning conference spaces into command centers and the higher-end suites into officer housing.

BIX CALEEN
Proprietor of the Caleen Salyard, Bix focuses on refurbished ion conversion nodes and related technology. She runs the place with her partner, Timm Karlo. While using a hidden communications node to sell unlicensed or prohibited salvage, she comes across a mysterious buyer willing to pay extra as long as Bix asks no questions. This stranger—Luthen Rael—opens to Bix a new world of rebellion.

Synth-leather tool belt and work apron

AM6B micro flame welder

The central thoroughfare of the city is Rix Road, forking at the bell tower that audibly marks the day's progress.

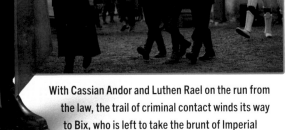

With Cassian Andor and Luthen Rael on the run from the law, the trail of criminal contact winds its way to Bix, who is left to take the brunt of Imperial attention and is arrested.

BRASSO

Loyal Brasso is an ideal example of the proud Ferrix grappler, tasked with breaking apart large wrecks to get at the valuable salvageable components within. He is a close friend of the Andor family.

FERRIXIANS

The Ferrixian economy depends on the continuous cycle of breakdown, salvage, repair, and resale, spawning a variety of additional careers and roles necessary to keep this close-knit society functioning.

PEGLA
LOT SENTRY

NURCHI
FREELANCE PICKER

TIMM KARLO
FLOOR MANAGER

XANWAN
FREIGHT DISPATCH

SALMAN PAAK
SALYARD BOSS

WILMON PAAK
SALYARD WORKER

MAARVA ANDOR

Maarva Carassi Andor is a lifelong Ferrixian, a skilled salvager, and a fixture in the community, serving as president of the Daughters of Ferrix—a social club. In her retirement, her neighbors look out for her as her health fails following a number of bitter winters. Maarva rescued a Kenari orphan, Kassa, from a restricted planet and doctored his records so that he would be known as Cassian Andor from Fest.

In death, Maarva's stirring words of freedom, direct action, and community inspire the Ferrixians into revolt against Imperial occupation.

CLEM ANDOR

Husband of Maarva Andor, Clem was skilled at finding the value in electronic refuse, using chemistry and elbow grease to buff it into near-new condition. Cassian still mourns his untimely death at the hands of the Empire.

Insulated work coveralls

CASSIAN ANDOR

A rebel able to forge what he needs to survive, Cassian Andor is at the crossroads of determining his own fate or drifting into self-destruction. Driven but without focus, Andor has a fierce temper and sense of justice burning within him, even if he has yet to find where best to apply his passion. His impulsivity leads him through a string of bad decisions and even worse luck, setting him on the run from corporate authorities.

Cassian desperately needs to escape and drag his problems away from Ferrix before they affect his loved ones. Luthen Rael becomes his ticket offworld, but into a more dangerous life of intrigue and revolution. He's no safer, but at least he has a cause beyond survival. Now, that redirected temper, honed by his skill and actions, has a chance to echo through history.

BANTHA TOY

Cassian is worlds away from his origins as Kassa, a boy stranded within a tribe of children on Kenari—a jungle world gripped by industrial disaster. He left his sister Kerri behind when he headed offworld with the Andors.

PRISON TRANSFORMATION

Cassian's unlawful incarceration at the Narkina 5 detention facility galvanizes him into becoming a leader of a prison revolt. He would rather die a rebel than toil away in service to the Empire. Cassian escapes from Narkina a changed man, and not long after commits to service as a rebel agent.

Adopted by Clem and Maarva Andor, Kassa becomes Cassian Jeron Andor, and Maarva's modest shack on Ferrix becomes an island of stability in his uprooted life.

Primary photoreceptor array

Expanding body sleeve

Storage tray

B2EMO

An aged groundmech droid used in salvage operations, loyal B2EMO ("Bee") is considered a valued member of the Andor family. His treads once tugged many kilograms of cargo, but his antiquated batteries now have trouble retaining a charge. Bee spends hours docked in his charging station, as complex processor operations—such as crafting a lie to cover for Cassian—drain his power reserves.

DATA FILE	
MANUFACTURER	Cybot Galactica
MODEL	B2 groundmech
TYPE	Salvage assist unit
HEIGHT	(typical) 0.73 m (2 ft 5 in); (fully extended) 0.79 m (2 ft 7 in)
WEAPONS	None
AFFILIATION	Andor family

High torque mobility treads

REBEL IN THE ROUGH

After his rescue from Kenari, Cassian had a difficult childhood adjusting to Ferrixian life. He spent much time in juvenile detention centers, including a three-year stint at Sipo. His teen years were also turbulent, coinciding with the rise of the Empire, but for all his trouble, the observant Cassian learns to survive.

DATA FILE

SUBJECT Cassian Jeron Andor

HOMEWORLD Kenari; Fest (birthplace as officially documented); Ferrix (adopted)

SPECIES Human

AFFILIATION Axis network

HEIGHT 1.78 m (5 ft 10 in)

AGE 27 (5 BBY)

Water-resistant carbamesh fabric

Coat patched after years of use

MW-20 Bryar heavy blaster pistol (formerly Clem Andor's)

> ## "I KNOW WHAT I'M AGAINST. EVERYTHING ELSE WILL HAVE TO WAIT."
> ### – CASSIAN ANDOR

Working belt with side-slung tool holster

FACT FILE

MIMBAN SERVICE
At age 16, Cassian serves as a cook for the ongoing Imperial campaign on Mimban, but later deserts.

LOST SISTER
Cassian chases down any leads of Kenari survivors in hopes of tracking down his sister Kerri, though Maarva implores him not to bother.

CORPORATE INTERESTS

Business interests in the Corporate Sector and beyond oversee vast swathes of territory, driving value for their shareholders. These corporations quickly fall in step with the Imperial regime, offering an extension of surveillance in exchange for unhindered pursuit of profit. This cooperative system usually works, but corporate missteps may prompt direct Imperial intervention and occupation. In the Free Trade Morlana Sector, the Consolidated Holdings of Preox-Morlana Corporation (or Pre-Mor for short) is the de facto government and police force.

SYRIL KARN

Ambitious and a true believer in rule of law, Syril Karn is an Imperial patriot. In truth, Karn's abilities are lackluster, and his career trajectory is shaped more by missteps and nepotism than by truly inspired leadership. Syril nonetheless is determined to achieve greatness, and hides his flaws behind intense loyalty and an impeccable polish in his wardrobe.

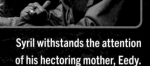

Syril withstands the attention of his hectoring mother, Eedy.

LINUS MOSK

A lowly sergeant in the Pre-Mor Authority Security Forces, Linus Mosk is inspired by Syril Karn's fervent adherence to procedure and protocol. Mosk has a marked distaste for disorder, and believes proactive monitoring and tactical enforcement is prudent policy.

Colored visors indicate squad leadership rank

Tac comlink in shoulder mount

Service-issue B1-NA blaster pistol

Insulated gloves

Plastoid poleyn

Slight tailoring on undertunic

Service-issue B1-NA is later in Ruescott Melshi's possession

Pre-Mor brand style guide blue

Flexi-mesh Mk 35 lightweight blast vest

Weatherproof expedition boots

DATA FILE

SUBJECT	Syril Karn
HOMEWORLD	Coruscant
SPECIES	Human
AFFILIATION	Preox Morlana Corporation
HEIGHT	1.78 m (5 ft 10 in)
AGE	35 years (5 BBY)

MORLANA ONE

The principal world of the Morlana system, and the corporate headquarters for Preox-Morlana, Morlana One is a dreary world of industry with a few bright spots found in cities that grew out of commercial housing. Pre-Mor Authority supplies all civil services to the citizens, or employees, on the planet, provided they log their hours appropriately and maintain adherence to compliance directives.

DATA FILE

REGION Outer Rim Territories

SECTOR Free Trade Morlana

SYSTEM Morlana

DIAMETER 11,236 km (6,982 miles)

TERRAIN
Oceans, coastal lowlands, and plains

MOONS 1

POPULATION 785 million

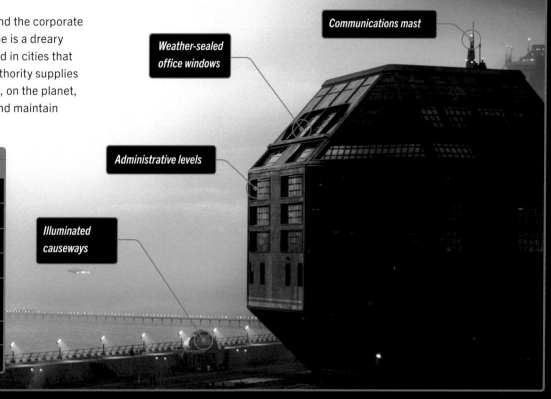

Communications mast

Weather-sealed office windows

Administrative levels

Illuminated causeways

PRE-MOR AUTHORITY CARRIER

The Pre-Mor Authority Patrol is a private fleet maintaining order within the Morlana sector. Dispatched from Morlana One, carriers are hyperspace-capable craft that ferry four mobile Tac-Pods for rapid deployment to troublesome spots. Each pod carries a squad of Tac-Corpos to the surface, while the carrier remains in low orbit.

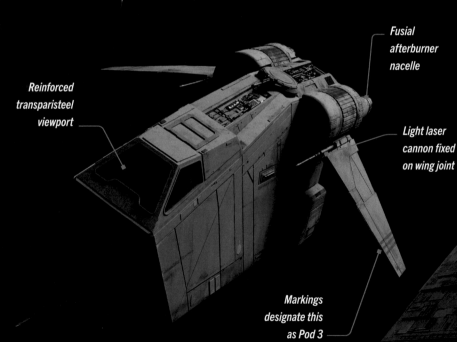

Fusial afterburner nacelle

Reinforced transparisteel viewport

Light laser cannon fixed on wing joint

Markings designate this as Pod 3

Starboard heavy laser cannon turret

Cockpit viewport slot

Orbital range transmitter mast

Tac-Pod 2 in stowed configuration

Double heavy laser cannon

Turret assembly

MOBILE TAC-POD

A compact landing craft, the mobile Tac-Pod has limited orbital range and relies on a larger carrier for distance travel. Its cramped interior can hold six Tac-Corpos, including the pilot. Though the vehicle does have a hull reinforced against small arms fire, it is not intended for use in combat scenarios.

AXIS NETWORK

"Axis" is an alias used by the Imperial Security Bureau (ISB) for a rebel spy who is otherwise nameless. Supervisor Dedra Meero is pulling together the web of clues into an increasingly cohesive picture as to who is at the center of this network. Cassian Andor emerges as a vital junction of motives and means, otherwise the driftless criminal would not have landed on ISB scanners. Just what could be Cassian's connection to the Aldhani heist?

In fact, it is Luthen Rael who is responsible. During this era of intrigue, Rael maintains a carefully crafted distance from his operations to remain unseen. His growing influence touches disparate rebel units, including the partisans under Saw Gerrera's leadership and Anto Kreegyr's separatist stalwarts. Rael remains an advisor who hovers just within earshot of these radicals, orchestrating operations and events while not setting foot into the worst of the battle zones.

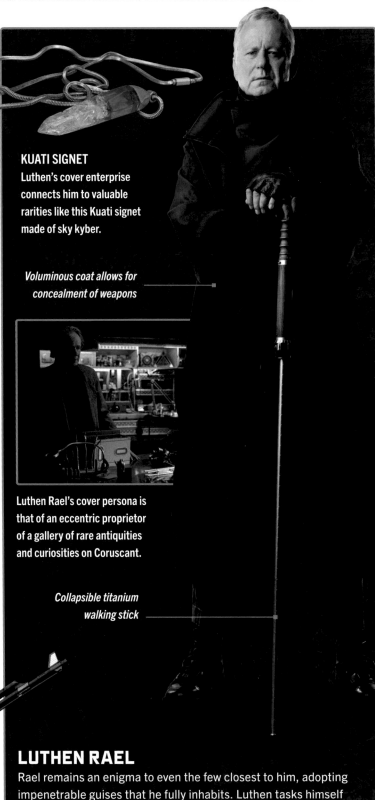

KUATI SIGNET
Luthen's cover enterprise connects him to valuable rarities like this Kuati signet made of sky kyber.

Voluminous coat allows for concealment of weapons

Luthen Rael's cover persona is that of an eccentric proprietor of a gallery of rare antiquities and curiosities on Coruscant.

Collapsible titanium walking stick

VEL SARTHA

Born into a Chandrilan life of privilege, Vel Sartha turns her back on an upscale upbringing to live in a more rustic and grounded way. This exposes her to many Imperial injustices and motivates her to become a rebel.

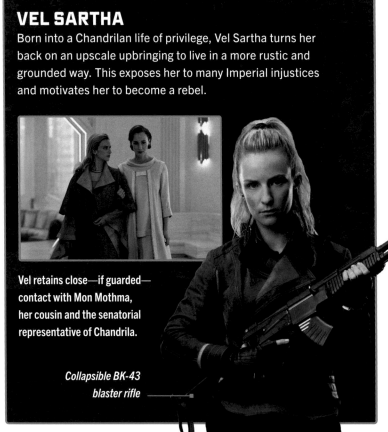

Vel retains close—if guarded—contact with Mon Mothma, her cousin and the senatorial representative of Chandrila.

Collapsible BK-43 blaster rifle

LUTHEN RAEL

Rael remains an enigma to even the few closest to him, adopting impenetrable guises that he fully inhabits. Luthen tasks himself to set in motion the downfall of the Empire, regardless of the personal compromises he must make, and compartmentalizes his life and mind to achieve his goals.

CINTA KAZ

A warrior, medic, and linguist, Cinta Kaz is dedicated to the cause and driven by tragedy. Her family was murdered by stormtroopers and she will not rest till the Empire is overthrown. Cinta prioritizes duty above all else, including her closest personal relationships.

KLEYA MARKI

More than just a gallery concierge and restorer, Kleya Marki is an impartial check against Rael's impulses and misjudgments. She warns Luthen when he overextends himself and reels him in with words of caution. Kleya may be the closest to Luthen and knows of his past before he embarked on his mission of revolution.

In the Imperial Senate, Mon Mothma champions causes meant to alleviate suffering and equalize opportunities across the Empire, often facing derision for misplaced sympathies.

Mon finds little support in her family life, as her traditionalist husband and daughter lack interest in her political career.

MON MOTHMA

The senior senatorial representative from Chandrila, Mon Mothma navigated the turmoil of the Clone Wars but now faces far more treacherous political waters during the era of Imperial peace. Mothma becomes a noticeable—if ineffective—political thorn in the side of the Emperor and a benign distraction in public, while secretly funding and facilitating rebellious actions. Regardless of which sphere she operates in, she lives up to the enlightened ideals of her homeworld.

Separate driver's compartment intended for privacy

Ventilation and turbojet intake port

Premium Quadrilayer-luster pearlescent finish

JPP-192 LIMOSPEEDER

Like most politicians, Mon Mothma relies on a personal chauffeur, as transit time is work time for the busy senator on the go. Her latest driver, Exmar Kloris, is an Imperial Security Bureau agent closely monitoring her words and actions. Mothma is aware of his allegiance and uses this knowledge to sow disinformation.

FONDOR HAULCRAFT

Like Luthen Rael, its pilot, the Fondor haulcraft is full of surprises and deception. At first glance it could be one of countless independent vessels hauling cargo for a living, but Luthen has arranged for extensive modifications and the addition of potent defenses and offensive weapon systems. Luthen's obsession with secrecy means he has eliminated support crew positions, instead relying on a droid intelligence to assist him in flight operations. Luthen clears its memory after each voyage.

Chaff launchers fire powerlessly with chemical propellants, invisible to enemy sensors

Starboard stabilizer and maneuvering thrusters

Continuous particle beam emitter (limited fire)

Secret layer of armor composite

Boarding ramp

Secret changing room

Docking tube

Heat dissipation matrix

DATA FILE

MANUFACTURER Fondor Yards Commercial Ventures	
MODEL V-21.1 Chevlex	
TYPE Light haulcraft	
DIMENSIONS Length: 25.82 m (84 ft 9 in); width (with wings out): 21.71 m (71 ft 3 in); height (with cannon deployed): 5.49 m (18 ft)	
WEAPONS 2 forward laser cannons; retractable antipersonnel laser cannons; dorsal double laser cannon turret; tandem continuous stream particle beam emitter; tractor beam projector; ballistic chaff launcher	
AFFILIATION Luthen Rael	

"WHAT'S POWERING THIS? I'VE BEEN IN A FONDOR HAULCRAFT. I'VE FLOWN THEM. NEVER SEEN ONE DO THAT."

– CASSIAN ANDOR

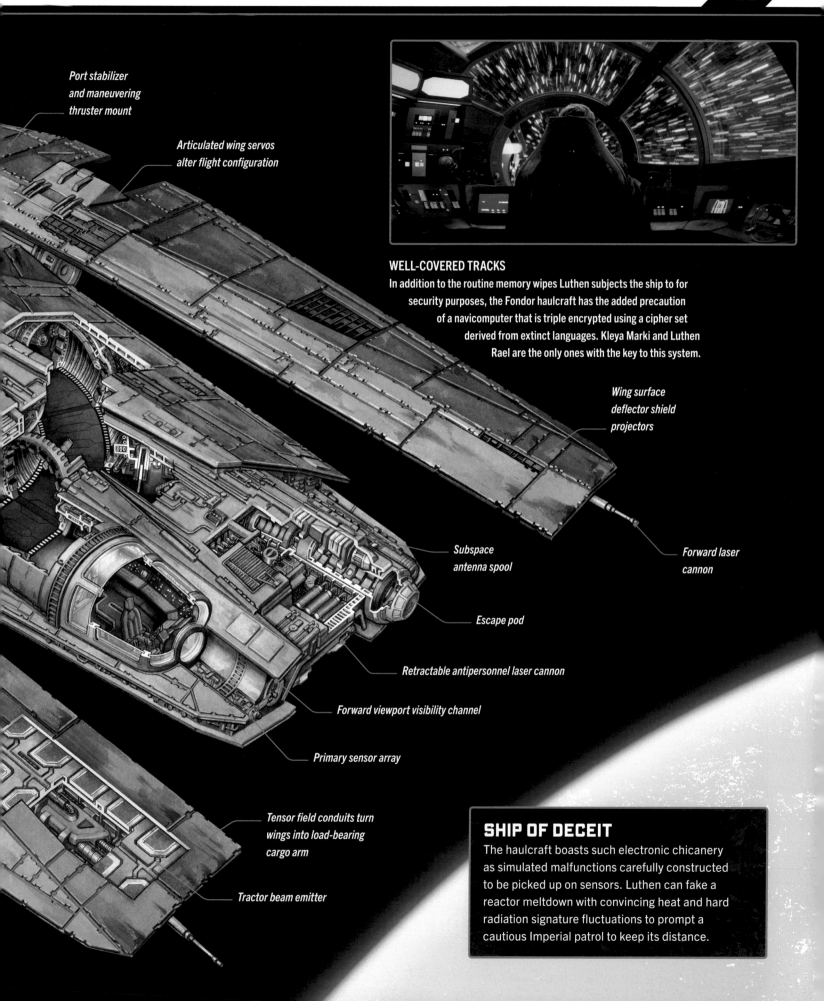

Port stabilizer
and maneuvering
thruster mount

Articulated wing servos
alter flight configuration

WELL-COVERED TRACKS

In addition to the routine memory wipes Luthen subjects the ship to for
security purposes, the Fondor haulcraft has the added precaution
of a navicomputer that is triple encrypted using a cipher set
derived from extinct languages. Kleya Marki and Luthen
Rael are the only ones with the key to this system.

Wing surface
deflector shield
projectors

Subspace
antenna spool

Forward laser
cannon

Escape pod

Retractable antipersonnel laser cannon

Forward viewport visibility channel

Primary sensor array

Tensor field conduits turn
wings into load-bearing
cargo arm

Tractor beam emitter

SHIP OF DECEIT

The haulcraft boasts such electronic chicanery
as simulated malfunctions carefully constructed
to be picked up on sensors. Luthen can fake a
reactor meltdown with convincing heat and hard
radiation signature fluctuations to prompt a
cautious Imperial patrol to keep its distance.

THE ISB

The Imperial Security Bureau (ISB) is the Empire's law enforcement agency that endeavors to root out treason. It is not the military, but can assume command of martial assets if deemed necessary for investigation. Army intelligence distrusts this organization, because a motivated ISB member could easily level a vindictive accusation against a decorated officer that would be hard to shake off. For this moment in history, as unrest grows, the ISB is on the rise and beyond censure.

The fallout of the Clone Wars resulted in incalculable damage wrought by the failure to predict Separatist intent and Jedi treachery. The formation of the Empire leads to an overhaul of the Republic's intelligence operations. Emperor Palpatine allows the ISB enormous leeway in interpreting threats and administrating solutions, riding the public's support and outcry for increased security. The Senate only knows a fraction of the ISB's true purview; agents use a wide variety of means to invade the privacy of Imperial citizens in the name of protection.

DEDRA MEERO

A rising officer within the ISB, Dedra Meero transfers from the Enforcement desk to Investigations. Her relatively young age and aggressive approach upsets the dull dynamic of ISB Central Office briefings. However, Dedra's initiative during an investigation into a stolen N-S9 starpath unit has gained the favorable eye of Major Partagaz.

Intact vector crystal matrix

N-S9 STARPATH UNIT

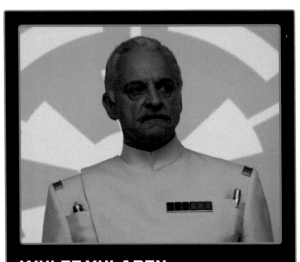

WULFF YULAREN

A decorated fleet admiral during the Clone Wars, Wulff Yularen transferred between service divisions; from the military and toward state surveillance. His former rank maps to his current position as colonel and his ISB position as director. His arrival at ISB Headquarters is met with a reception fit for the Emperor himself.

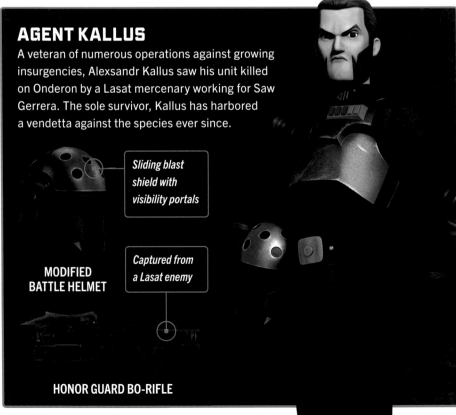

AGENT KALLUS

A veteran of numerous operations against growing insurgencies, Alexsandr Kallus saw his unit killed on Onderon by a Lasat mercenary working for Saw Gerrera. The sole survivor, Kallus has harbored a vendetta against the species ever since.

Sliding blast shield with visibility portals

MODIFIED BATTLE HELMET

Captured from a Lasat enemy

HONOR GUARD BO-RIFLE

ISB CENTRAL OFFICE

LIO PARTAGAZ
A severe official tolerating no failure under his command, Major Partagaz reminds his supervisors of the ISB's mandate and importance in stability.

SUPERVISOR JUNG
Supervisor Lonni Jung harbors a secret from the rest of the ISB: he is a double agent feeding information to Luthen Rael.

SUPERVISOR BLEVIN
By-the-manuals to the extreme, Supervisor Blevin is an unimaginative officer who hides in the details of bureaucracy when advantageous.

ATTENDANT HEERT
A staffer working for Dedra Meero, Attendant Heert shares many of her views and works tirelessly to help her get ahead.

LISTENING SHIP

An IGV-55 surveillance vessel is one of the many tools the Empire has at its command to spy on citizens. The modified Gozanti cruiser bristles with signal interception hardware, most notably the sensor dome on its dorsal surface. Dedicated crewers, who have undergone Lobot-Tech brace surgery to enhance their brains at the cost of their personality, maximize the vessel's effectiveness.

Active phased FST (full spectrum transceiver) array

Passive DER (dedicated energy receptor) array

Twin laser cannon (rear-arc coverage)

Sublight ion turbine insulated to prevent interference

Sensor dish houses high-resolution spinning HSI receiver

EM-insulated bridge module

Composite hull coating to minimize signal leakage

Ventral entry platform

Landing gear

ALWAYS WATCHING
Controller LT-319 is the operations manager aboard an IGV-55 near Killun Station. He monitors intercepted transmissions for rebel leads.

DATA FILE

MANUFACTURER	Corellian Engineering Corporation
MODEL	IGV-55 *Gozanti*-class
TYPE	Surveillance vessel
DIMENSIONS	Length: 62.75 m (205 ft 11 in); width: 36.66 m (120 ft 3 in); height: 21.95 m (72 ft)
WEAPONS	Two heavy laser cannons
AFFILIATION	Galactic Empire

ALDHANI HEIST

The remote world of Aldhani is transforming under a cruel administration. Unique sensor-baffling geological qualities of nearby caverns and exposure to orbital micro-crystal deposits draw the Empire to the planet. Over the course of 13 years, 40,000 Dhani highlanders have been cleared from the sacred valleys, funneled into newly built lowland towns where they work in factories intended to remodel their home into a major Imperial resource.

Recruited under extreme duress to undertake a very risky assignment, Cassian Andor poses as "Clem" on a mission to heist an Imperial payroll at an understaffed garrison on Aldhani. A window of opportunity beckons, as the triennial phenomenon named the Mak-ani bray Dhani, also known as "the Eye" in Galactic Basic, approaches, promising enough atmospheric disruption and spectacle to serve as cover for a daring infiltration.

The strike team disguise themselves from distant view as ghoat-herders—local people who are some of the last of the rustic Dhani highlanders to still roam the hills.

KARIS NEMIK

Not outwardly martial, Karis Nemik is nonetheless an essential part of the Aldhani operation. Karis is a brilliant astronavigator, having studied Columi and Givin theoretics that allow him to make manual calculations at rapid speeds. He carries with him a primitive, pre-Empire astronave for complex formulations, a device insulated from Imperial observation. His is a young mind eager for new information and challenges.

Nemik's curiosity draws him to explore political theory. He collects his thoughts into a growing manifesto within a datapad, offering guidance to would-be revolutionaries.

Dhani scarf protects against highland winds

Red marks the cleansing fire of the Eye ritual

Traditional homespun ghoat wool

Nemik is drawn to Cassian, for he sees someone who is eager to learn as well as worthy of study. In time, Cassian appreciates Nemik's treatises on rebellion.

RONO HAULER

The crystalline deposits that make Aldhani valuable to the Empire reduce the reliability of repulsorlift systems. Positional repulsors and acceleration compensators are affected within the Nasma Klain river valley, necessitating the reliance on the launch base at Alkenzi for air support. A rail-mounted Rono freighter overcomes these complications, and becomes a central target of the heist.

The launch bay has been tailor-made for the track-guided launch. Cassian's familiarity with such systems is essential to the mission.

High-density aurodium ingots pre-packed in carry cylinders are the prize of the heist; even a partial haul promises millions of credits.

The Mak-ani bray Dhani occurs as Aldhani passes through a trail of noctilucent micro-crystalline fragments in its orbit.

DATA FILE

MANUFACTURER Sienar Fleet Systems	
MODEL Max-7 Rono	
TYPE Box freighter, rail-launched	
DIMENSIONS Length: 29.74 m (97 ft 7 in); width: 8.78 m (28 ft 10 in); height: 7.35 m (24 ft 1 in)	
WEAPONS None	
AFFILIATION Galactic Empire	

A lack of acceleration compensators makes launches an arduous event for crews not used to pulling G-forces. Cargo aboard must be securely fastened, as loose items become a potential threat.

ARVEL SKEEN

There's the story Arvel Skeen tells regarding his fight against the Empire; and then there is the truth, which he keeps to himself. His body also tells a story, thanks to the presence of numerous prison tattoos. He is a mercurial man who struggles to trust Cassian Andor.

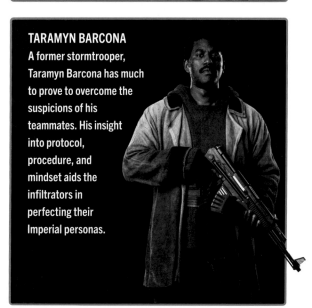

TARAMYN BARCONA

A former stormtrooper, Taramyn Barcona has much to prove to overcome the suspicions of his teammates. His insight into protocol, procedure, and mindset aids the infiltrators in perfecting their Imperial personas.

LIEUTENANT GORN

The person on the inside of the heist operation, Gorn has been posted to Aldhani for seven years. During this time he falls in love with a local woman, which earns him a reprimand from his superiors.

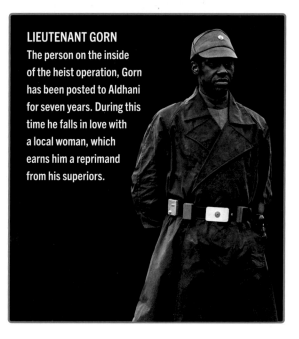

SAW GERRERA

The ally in one generation may be the enemy in the next, says an old Atrisian maxim. Saw Gerrera embodies it well. As a young man, Gerrera was armed and trained by the Republic to do battle with the Separatists in a proxy war on Onderon. Feeling betrayed by the Republic as it transforms into the Empire, Saw keeps fighting, but targets the Empire instead. He leads a band of extremist partisans in sudden and terrifying strikes against vulnerable targets, heedless of the collateral damage involved.

Saw has long been competitive in spirit, which added to his charm as a young man. During the Clone Wars he was more aggressive than his colleagues, and would butt heads with his sister, Steela Gerrera. While she wanted to unite the citizens of Onderon and win their hearts and minds, Saw desired—above all—to make the enemy hurt. When Saw's sister died in an attack on the rebel base, the last threads that anchored his compassion were snapped and he effectively lost his conscience.

REBEL FROM THE START

Like many local resistance fighters, Saw was skeptical of Republic aid during the Clone Wars, fearful that he would be trading one occupying force for another. Such concern was prescient, as the emergent Empire lays claim to Onderon. Saw and his fellow fighters retreat to the jungle, forming a brigade of partisans that would attack the Empire for years across many worlds.

STRIKE ON ONOAM

Saw strikes with no concern for the lives of citizens. On Naboo's moon of Onoam, he orders the bombing of Moff Panaka's chalet, nearly killing the visiting Princess Leia Organa.

A HARD LIFE

ONDERONIAN STRIFE
A friendly fire incident from Saw himself resulted in the death of Steela during the Clone Wars.

NO BACKING DOWN
The Empire dispatches Clone Force 99 to rein in the partisans on Onderon, but Saw won't relent.

ERIADU STRIKE
Saw and his partisans infiltrate an Imperial conference on Eriadu, jeopardizing a simultaneous mission carried out by the Bad Batch.

PARTISAN AGITATOR
Imperial pressure forces Saw to hide in inhospitable environs. Saw's actions cause him to find little assistance in the growing rebellion.

GEONOSIAN OBSESSION
In his strikes against the Empire, Saw begins to suspect that the Imperials are constructing something abominable. His search leads him to Geonosis.

CRYSTAL CHASE
More clues guide Saw to realize that kyber crystals are key to whatever the Empire is building.

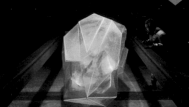

JEDHA LAIR
The search leads Saw to the Pilgrim Moon of Jedha, a natural trove of kyber crystals and the site of a heavy Imperial presence.

CLARITY OF PURPOSE

Saw has lost much in two decades of combat, but rare flashes of the charismatic and caring man he once was shine through. To wartime scholars, Saw represents the poison of violence and warfare; how someone who has been exposed to too much conflict can have their humanity burned away by it. In an era hungry for heroes and inspiration, Saw cares little for how history will record his deeds, provided that he succeeds.

DISTRUSTFUL ALLIANCE

Saw's take-no-prisoners approach resonates well with Luthen Rael's pragmatic view of rebellion, though Luthen's methods are more subtle than Saw's bombastic approach. Their intense paranoia prevents them from forming a lasting alliance.

DATA FILE

SUBJECT	Saw Gerrera
HOMEWORLD	Onderon
SPECIES	Human
AFFILIATION	Partisan leader
HEIGHT	1.8 m (5 ft 11 in)
AGE	Unknown (records destroyed)

Vac-suit hermetic coupler

DH-16 blaster with perforated cooling sleeve

Sealing wrist cuff

Corrugated vac-suit articulation

"I HOPE, SENATOR, AFTER YOU'VE LOST AND THE EMPIRE REIGNS OVER THE GALAXY UNOPPOSED, YOU WILL FIND SOME COMFORT IN THE KNOWLEDGE THAT YOU FOUGHT ACCORDING TO THE RULES."

– SAW GERRERA TO MON MOTHMA

By the time the Death Star project becomes known to the Rebel Alliance, Saw is a dying man, kept alive by machinery.

PARTISANS

Before long, Saw Gerrera's movement grows beyond his fellow Onderonian veterans as word of his strikes against the Empire spreads. In the Outer Rim, far from the policing eyes of the Senate, the Empire embraces its most extreme acts of draconian rule. These worlds produce battle-scarred survivors eager to join Saw in his quest for justice and vengeance.

Novaldex Diagnostech pilot's life support unit

Breathing apparatus for survival in oxygen-rich atmospheres

FACT FILE

WELCOME MISDIRECTION
Unaffiliated opportunists copying Saw's violent methods and claiming to be "partisans" sow confusion in both Imperial and rebel intelligence ranks. Gerrera applauds such imitation if effective.

A HIGH PRICE
The penalty for disloyalty among the partisans is summary execution.

EDRIO TWO-TUBES

As a member of the Tognath diaspora, Edrio becomes a mercenary known to be a crack sharpshooter. Edrio earns credits and a reputation as a big-game hunter on worlds without sentient life. He charges the wealthy and privileged for the thrill of seemingly dangerous safaris. After Edrio ensures a notable Imperial Moff does not survive a spell of adventure tourism, he attracts the attention of Saw Gerrera.

BENTHIC TWO-TUBES

Yar Togna is brutally conquered by the Empire early in its reign, scattering Tognath refugees to the spacelanes. Benthic's hunger for revenge is only rivaled by his drive to find his missing "eggmate" brother, Edrio. Drifting in mercenary circles, Benthic spends time as part of Enfys Nest's band of Cloud-Rider marauders, where he gains the nickname "Tubes." After his reunion with his eggmate in the partisans, this moniker changes to "Two-Tubes" and is shared with Edrio.

Weatherproof retailored diaphanous Tognathian extruded fabric

Long barrel with enhanced galven circuitry produces bolts with extended range and coherence

DATA FILE

SUBJECT	Benthic and Edrio Two-Tubes
HOMEWORLD	Yar Togna
SPECIES	Tognath
AFFILIATION	Partisan
HEIGHT	1.9 m (6 ft 3 in)
AGE	27 (5 BBY)

Utility belt pouches with ammunition packs

Rifle butt of carved wroshyr wood

Tognath feet crammed into human-issue boots

Benthic favors a duster jacket picked up in the Aduba system

JYN ERSO

Saw Gerrera is instrumental in extracting scientist Galen Erso and his family from the Empire's grip. When Imperials recapture Galen, Saw rescues Erso's daughter, Jyn, and proceeds to raise her as his own with an odd mix of tender care and harsh drills. As suspicions about her parentage grow among the partisans, Saw leaves 16-year-old Jyn for her own safety, deeming her ready to survive on her own.

MIAM LYMONTRA

Miam Lymontra has a bounty on her head for her part in the riots protesting Imperial sanctions on Ingo. She convinces the partisans that she is worth more as a fighter than the credits they could collect via a proxy.

KULLBEE SPERADO

A laconic gunslinger recruited by Gerrera on Serralonis, Kullbee Sperado keeps to himself, figuring correctly that there's always a fool eager to fill silence with unneeded noise.

DAFIR TOOGAN

A mechanic, Dafir Toogan attempts to maintain the chronically malfunctioning Cavern Angel squadron. Exposure to fuel and coolant chemicals requires him to wear a hermetic breath mask.

CASITINE LOSCAR

A scout on Jedha, Casitine Loscar has several face-concealing disguises he wears while navigating the crowded marketplace, eavesdropping for any valuable intel. The partisans call this helmeted look "Tin Head."

RENLO WAIMET

Part of the security detail at Segra Milo, Renlo Waimet has an understandable mistrust of outsiders. He believes Saw should have nothing to do with the larger rebellion.

JAVROTH MEERS

Following an arrest for assault by the Milvayne Authority, Javroth Meers escapes by knocking out an officer and stealing their uniform. Meers now wears the outfit as a badge of rebellion.

MOROFF

Despite claims of being apolitical, the mercenary Moroff shows a tenacious loyalty to Saw Gerrera even when pickings are slim. The towering Gigoran serves as a heavy gunner on Jedha.

AZUDO CHANCH

A Cavern Angel pilot and also an able mechanic, Azudo Chanch wears cobbled-together kit that includes the facemask of an Imperial scout trooper.

JOALI ANDIT

Half of a married mercenary team alongside his wife Jalice, Joali Andit is an adrenaline-fueled thrill-seeker. He comes to Jedha City specifically looking for conflict.

PARTISAN BASES

Saw Gerrera's troops are used to roughing it, living with few amenities while surviving off the land. From outposts hidden within the jungle ruins of Onderon to the deep abandoned mines of Segra Milo, Saw's partisans exhibit a talent for seeking out defendable strongholds that are uncomfortable, unappealing, and little known. These harsh conditions function as a first line of defense: few would willingly want to make the trip.

CONNECTED HEADQUARTERS

Though Saw's trappings are rustic, he maintains a command center filled with equipment looted from corporate and Imperial raids. Encoded communications bases allow Saw to tap into HoloNet nodes, keeping him up to date with the latest galactic developments.

JEDHA BASE

Saw's obsession with uncovering just what the Empire is doing with kyber crystals leads him to the Pilgrim Moon of Jedha. He sets up camp in the Catacombs of Cadera, an ancient structure battered by time and the elements. The locals in nearby Jedha City give the site a wide berth as they claim it is haunted. This handy superstition lets Saw keep his privacy and monitor the Empire at a distance.

Old mine entrance leads to command center

Sensor repeater pod

BOR GULLET

Mairans, also known as mind flayers, are large, sentient cephalopods that can compel their prey to tell the truth through prolonged exposure to their embrace. However, the victim will start to lose some of their memories. Thanks to this gruesome skill, the Mairan Bor Gullet serves as Saw's interrogator on Jedha.

SEGRA MILO

A barren, miserable planet with abandoned caverns and played-out mines, Segra Milo is the site of a partisan starfighter launch base. When a nearby commercial trade post starts complaining of pirate activity in the neighboring sector, the Empire steps up patrols near Segra Milo, causing Saw to contemplate a costly relocation.

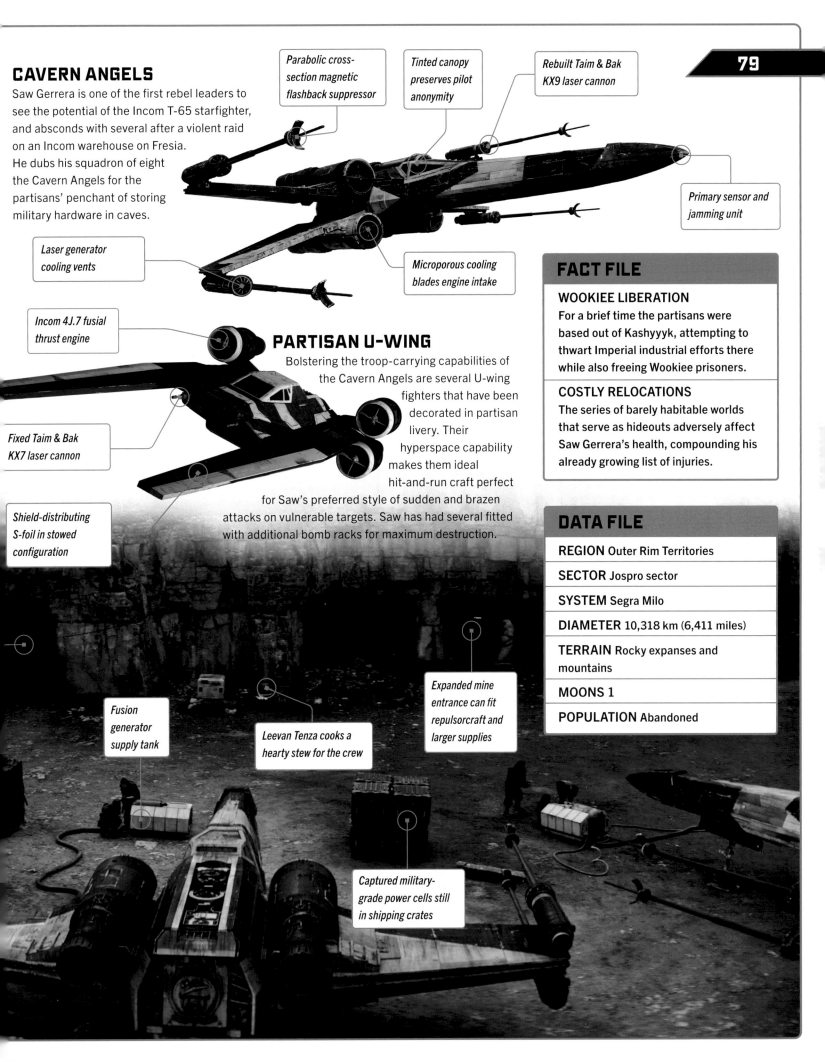

CAVERN ANGELS

Saw Gerrera is one of the first rebel leaders to see the potential of the Incom T-65 starfighter, and absconds with several after a violent raid on an Incom warehouse on Fresia. He dubs his squadron of eight the Cavern Angels for the partisans' penchant of storing military hardware in caves.

Parabolic cross-section magnetic flashback suppressor

Tinted canopy preserves pilot anonymity

Rebuilt Taim & Bak KX9 laser cannon

Primary sensor and jamming unit

Laser generator cooling vents

Microporous cooling blades engine intake

Incom 4J.7 fusial thrust engine

PARTISAN U-WING

Bolstering the troop-carrying capabilities of the Cavern Angels are several U-wing fighters that have been decorated in partisan livery. Their hyperspace capability makes them ideal hit-and-run craft perfect for Saw's preferred style of sudden and brazen attacks on vulnerable targets. Saw has had several fitted with additional bomb racks for maximum destruction.

Fixed Taim & Bak KX7 laser cannon

Shield-distributing S-foil in stowed configuration

Fusion generator supply tank

Leevan Tenza cooks a hearty stew for the crew

Expanded mine entrance can fit repulsorcraft and larger supplies

Captured military-grade power cells still in shipping crates

FACT FILE

WOOKIEE LIBERATION

For a brief time the partisans were based out of Kashyyyk, attempting to thwart Imperial industrial efforts there while also freeing Wookiee prisoners.

COSTLY RELOCATIONS

The series of barely habitable worlds that serve as hideouts adversely affect Saw Gerrera's health, compounding his already growing list of injuries.

DATA FILE

REGION	Outer Rim Territories
SECTOR	Jospro sector
SYSTEM	Segra Milo
DIAMETER	10,318 km (6,411 miles)
TERRAIN	Rocky expanses and mountains
MOONS	1
POPULATION	Abandoned

REBEL COMMANDERS

Alliance High Command shapes the overall flow of the rebel efforts in the galaxy. It allocates resources and coordinates intelligence to maximum effect, and the Rebellion lives or dies based on the skills of the leaders in their scattered cells. These brave individuals come from a wide variety of backgrounds. Veterans from the Clone Wars, Republic and Separatist alike, have joined the cause—united by opposition to the Empire. Officials within the Imperial government defect to the growing Alliance, bringing with them valuable knowledge. Planetary leaders preemptively stand up before their worlds are occupied.

Leadership in the face of such overwhelming odds takes distinct courage. Unlike the Imperial military, there is no academy program producing rebel officers. Instead, this more individualized reality—whereby rebel leadership invariably has deeply personal reasons to revolt—produces stronger examples of valor and vision. A Maya Pei separatist fighting song says of the Empire: "They fight because they are told to; we fight because we have to."

Commander Jun Sato leads an intelligence briefing with members of the Spectre team and Fulcrum agent Ahsoka Tano.

AHSOKA TANO

A former Padawan who walked away from the Jedi Order before the end of the Clone Wars, Ahsoka Tano is an outcast and survivor of Order 66. Through contact with Bail Organa, she spearheads a rebel recruitment and supply network under the code name "Fulcrum." She also helps spirit Force-sensitive children away from the Inquisitorius. Ahsoka mysteriously vanishes after a catastrophic mission to Malachor.

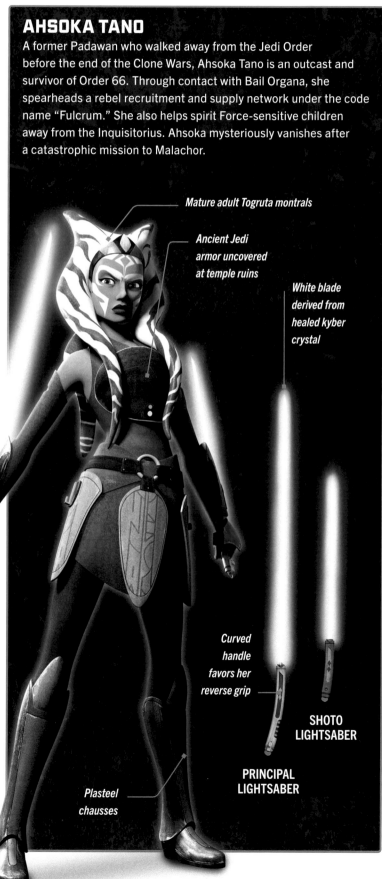

Mature adult Togruta montrals

Ancient Jedi armor uncovered at temple ruins

White blade derived from healed kyber crystal

Curved handle favors her reverse grip

SHOTO LIGHTSABER

PRINCIPAL LIGHTSABER

Plasteel chausses

SENATOR PAMLO

A vocal senator opposed to the increased militarization of the Empire, Tynnra Pamlo of Taris is also secretly a member of Alliance High Command. She helps expose Imperial atrocities and tailor the Alliance's messages to counter the blatant fearmongering of the Empire's anti-rebel rhetoric.

Rex makes covert contact with Clone Force 99, the Bad Batch.

Shoulder pauldron displaying 501st clone battalion livery

Battered helmet is a welded blend of Phase I and Phase II designs

JUN SATO

The leader of the Phoenix rebel cell, Jun Sato was part of Mykapo's planetary defense forces before moving onto the larger Rebellion. He is by-the-manual in his approach to warfare, and the undisciplined style of the Spectre crew does on occasion rankle him.

REX

Formerly a clone officer, Rex (CT-7567) barely escapes the Clone Wars in one piece, nearly succumbing to the brain-altering neural inhibitor chip that triggers Order 66 and turns so many of his fellow troopers into Jedi-killers. A fugitive in the time of the Empire, Rex's mission is to uncover the Imperial agenda as it pertains to the future of the clone army.

GIAL ACKBAR

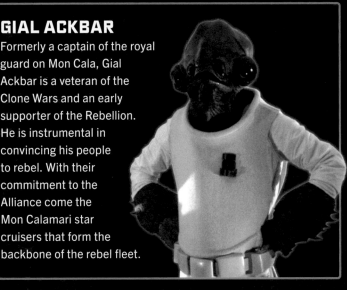

Formerly a captain of the royal guard on Mon Cala, Gial Ackbar is a veteran of the Clone Wars and an early supporter of the Rebellion. He is instrumental in convincing his people to rebel. With their commitment to the Alliance come the Mon Calamari star cruisers that form the backbone of the rebel fleet.

NIGHTSWAN

A former smuggler and pirate, Nevil Cygni gains newfound purpose as an insurgent leader under the alias Nightswan. He is a cunning tactician, fomenting crises on worlds such as Umbara, Cyphar, and Batonn. Nightswan is ultimately thwarted by a clever up-and-coming Imperial officer named Thrawn.

REBEL CELLS

The danger of Imperial reprisal means that early rebel operatives need to work in compartmentalized units called cells. The definition is quite broad: a cell can be a single operative eavesdropping on Imperial communications and forwarding valuable intel; or a militia of insurrectionists waging a guerilla war against an Imperial governor. The uniting principles include an intentionally limited connection to the larger rebellion to minimize damage from capture and interrogation.

CELLS AND FACTIONS

The early Rebellion is rife with loosely defined units and conflicting classifications. Before the coalescing of the Alliance proper, factions only cooperate with and aid other cells in order to achieve a larger objective; however, such overcoming of distrust is rare. Among the factions in these uncertain times are Maya Pei's Neo-Republican Collective, Saw Gerrera's partisans, the Atrivis Resistance Group, the Fakir Roughnecks, the Ghorman Front, and the Bellassan Galaxy Petitionists.

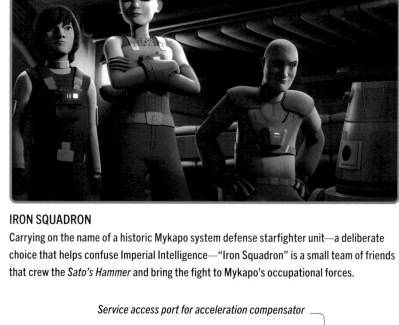

IRON SQUADRON
Carrying on the name of a historic Mykapo system defense starfighter unit—a deliberate choice that helps confuse Imperial Intelligence—"Iron Squadron" is a small team of friends that crew the *Sato's Hammer* and bring the fight to Mykapo's occupational forces.

Service access port for acceleration compensator

Modified Kuat Vonak A2-C dorsal laser turret

SATO'S HAMMER

Cockpit fore of the evacuation corridor and primary escape pod

THE *STINGER MANTIS* CREW

The crew of the *Stinger Mantis* includes the pilot Greez Dritus, Nightsister exile Merrin, explorer droid BD-1, and Jedi survivors Cal Kestis and Cere Junda. The team partakes in a variety of missions to save fugitives of the Empire and vex the Inquisitorius.

DATA FILE

MANUFACTURER	Corellian Engineering Corporation
MODEL	YT-2400
TYPE	Light freighter
DIMENSIONS	Length: 23.84 m (78 ft 3 in); width: 31.75 m (104 ft 2 in); height: 6.45 m (21 ft 2 in)
WEAPONS	2 double laser turrets; concussion missile launchers
AFFILIATION	Iron Squadron

ANTO KREEGYR

A stalwart Confederate holdout who becomes a leading figure in the neo-Separatist Coalition seeking legitimacy in the eyes of the Senate, Anto Kreegyr has been likened to an ox for his stubbornness. His cell seeks independence from the Empire above all else, and plans an assault on the Imperial power station on Spellhaus. Testament to the disposable nature of even powerful rebel cells, Luthen Rael sacrifices Kreegyr and his unit to protect the security of a mole within the ISB.

Departing Corellia aboard their ship, the *Silver Angel*, Trace and Rafa communicate valuable information to Rex, a clone survivor and early rebel.

Trace's self-tailored flight jacket

Faux tuggle-fur coat

THE MARTEZ SISTERS

Trace and Rafa Martez were originally up-and-coming smugglers from Level 1313 of Coruscant's lower depths. A run-in with a former Jedi and, later, a clone survivor, puts them on a clearer moral path of opposing the Empire. They offer up their undercity garage as a meeting space for rebels.

AMIDALANS

Founded by former royal handmaiden Sabé, the Amidalans are a cell of fellow handmaidens and other loyal individuals with the very specific focus of uncovering the truth of Padmé Amidala's mysterious death. In their quest for answers and justice, the Amidalans also thwart other Imperial activities while maintaining a veil of secrecy.

TARFFUL

A veteran of the Clone Wars, Tarfful has watched with growing rage as the once helpful Republic turns into the Empire that subjugates his people. From the densely wooded Shadowlands, this Wookiee chieftain leads destructive strikes against Imperial occupational forces.

Long-gun crafted on Kashyyyk

R7-A7

Formerly Ahsoka Tano's astromech in the Clone Wars, R7-A7 has been refurbished and reprogrammed to aid the Martez sisters.

Stowed spacecraft linkage and control arms

ZARE LEONIS

An Imperial cadet and rebel informant at the stormtrooper academy on Lothal, Zare Leonis is driven to find his vanished Force-sensitive sister, Dhara.

Cadet helmet

CAL KESTIS
Order 66 survivor and former Jedi Padawan Cal Kestis keeps a low profile working as a rigger in the Scrapper Guild on Bracca. A desperate demonstration of his Force abilities while saving a colleague draws the attention of the Inquisitorius, turning Cal into a fugitive once more. The young Jedi finds allies while on the run—including his loyal explorer droid, BD-1.

LOTHAL

The Empire has multiple reasons to target the provincial Outer Rim world of Lothal. It occupies the planet not only for its rich mineral wealth, which could be turned into military materiel, but also to establish Lothal as a navigational point on a new hyperspace path further into the Outer Rim. There are also more mystical reasons, as the world itself is the site of a potentially unique Force vergence (a location where Force sensitives may interact with the Force in potent ways).

DATA FILE

REGION	Outer Rim Territories
SECTOR	Lothal
SYSTEM	Lothal
DIAMETER	11,534 km (7,169 miles)
TERRAIN	Grasslands, low mountains, tundra, ocean
MOONS	2
POPULATION	285 million

Northern tundra, site of an ancient Jedi temple

Dinar settlement

Kinpany Gap mining settlement

ARIHNDA PRYCE

Governor Arihnda Pryce is the top Imperial authority on Lothal, tasked with keeping the Empire's many operations on the planet running smoothly. Though a competent manager, she is not equipped to deal with subversive activities under her stewardship. Desperation makes her increasingly dangerous.

Military uniform granted to civilian command

Capital City

LOTH-WOLVES

Lothalites think that Loth-wolves are extinct. However, a small pack of the canids lives in the planet's northern latitudes. Loth-wolves are the subject of many legends, as they are believed to possess mystical abilities.

LOTHAL LOCATIONS

JEDI TEMPLE
This Jedi temple protects an entryway to a strange vergence in the Force, a gateway to an ethereal plane. Jedi relics are also housed within.

EZRA'S ROOST
Young Ezra Bridger squats in an abandoned communications tower which he has turned into his home. Sabine Wren will inherit this dwelling.

OLD JHO'S
Old Jho's is a bar and eatery in the Lothal spaceport, named after its friendly Ithorian owner. It is a favored place to unwind.

REBEL BASE
A small, temporary encampment used by local resistance fighters led by Ryder Azadi, this site is tucked in the northern mountains.

CAPITAL CITY
The bustling civic hub of Lothal, the planet's capital has local merchants, industrial facilities, and gleaming white skyscrapers. The Imperial presence establishes a dome-shaped command headquarters from which all operations are planned. The coastal city draws in water to cool and power the busy Imperial projects underway.

IMPERIAL OCCUPATION
For the denizens of Capital City, the Imperial occupation on Lothal is predominantly realized by factory work producing the Empire's war materiel. The Imperial-aligned company Sienar Fleet Systems has a sizable presence on Lothal.

RYDER AZADI
The governor of Lothal prior to the occupation, Ryder Azadi was imprisoned by the Empire. Breaking free and returning to his homeworld, Azadi leads a local resistance against the Imperials.

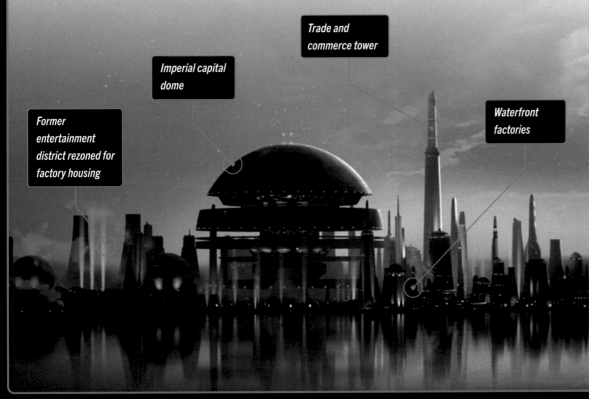

Trade and commerce tower

Imperial capital dome

Former entertainment district rezoned for factory housing

Waterfront factories

Goldgrass flaxen fabric scarf

Traditional northerner garb

LOTHAL REBELS

The insurgency on Lothal begins small, with a close-knit cell of operatives organized by Hera Syndulla. Tasked by Bail Organa and agent Fulcrum (Ahsoka Tano) with keeping a close watch on the growing Imperial presence on Lothal, Hera leads the Spectre team in a series of successful missions.

In time, their victories draw the attention of Grand Moff Tarkin, who is responsible for bringing order to the unruly Outer Rim. Not wanting to subject Lothal to brutal reprisals, the Spectres withdraw for a while to operate in nearby systems before returning to the pastoral planet to secure its freedom. In their victory, the Spectres operate apart from the larger Rebellion, as their objectives grow increasingly personal.

The Spectres go on to destroy the Imperial headquarters and break the blockading fleet through extremely unorthodox maneuvers. It's a victory the Empire is more willing to attribute to Governor Pryce's incompetence than any real rebel ingenuity. Whether or not the story of the rebellion on Lothal is truly over or merely paused while the focus of the Galactic Civil War spreads elsewhere remains to be seen.

Sabine Wren paints this mural following the liberation of Lothal, commemorating the Spectres, including those who are now lost.

HERA SYNDULLA

A true believer in the causes of freedom, liberty, and equality, Hera Syndulla is the leader of the Spectres, though by design she is content to let people believe Kanan is in charge. She has a keen eye for seeing potential in others and mentoring them to bring out their best.

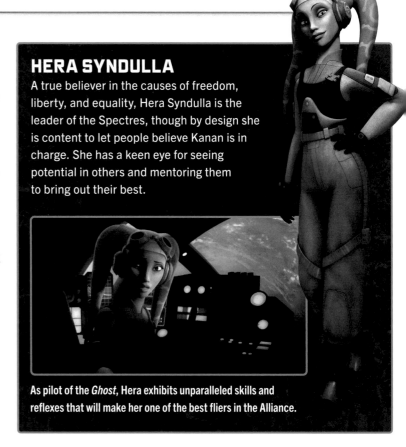

As pilot of the *Ghost*, Hera exhibits unparalleled skills and reflexes that will make her one of the best fliers in the Alliance.

KANAN JARRUS

Formerly known as Caleb Dume, Kanan Jarrus was but a Padawan when Order 66 destroyed the only life he knew. He spends years on the run, hiding his Jedi heritage to survive. Drawn to Hera's idealism, Kanan makes an excellent partner to her as part of the Spectres. Hunted by Inquisitors, Kanan's life as a Jedi survivor is hard.

Kanan returns to his Jedi ways as he takes on an unconventional apprentice, Ezra Bridger, to pass on his knowledge of the Force to.

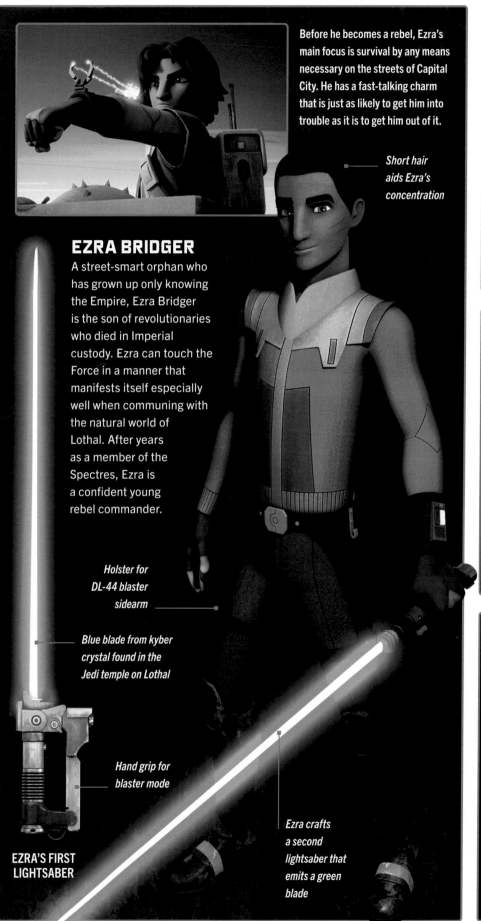

Before he becomes a rebel, Ezra's main focus is survival by any means necessary on the streets of Capital City. He has a fast-talking charm that is just as likely to get him into trouble as it is to get him out of it.

Short hair aids Ezra's concentration

EZRA BRIDGER

A street-smart orphan who has grown up only knowing the Empire, Ezra Bridger is the son of revolutionaries who died in Imperial custody. Ezra can touch the Force in a manner that manifests itself especially well when communing with the natural world of Lothal. After years as a member of the Spectres, Ezra is a confident young rebel commander.

Holster for DL-44 blaster sidearm

Blue blade from kyber crystal found in the Jedi temple on Lothal

Hand grip for blaster mode

EZRA'S FIRST LIGHTSABER

Ezra crafts a second lightsaber that emits a green blade

SABINE WREN

A headstrong Mandalorian, Sabine Wren is a gifted artist and an energetic saboteur. As a teen prodigy, she develops weaponry at the Imperial academy on Mandalore. She is expressive and colorful, with a passion for technology and explosives. Sabine is very independent-minded.

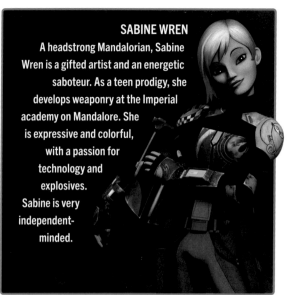

CHOPPER

A surly older model astromech, Chopper is crabby and recalcitrant. Hera has known him for years and has gotten used to his unfriendly personality. Despite his gripes, Chopper is ever reliable.

Sensor/transmitter dish

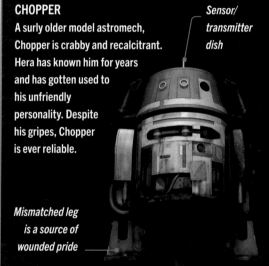

Mismatched leg is a source of wounded pride

Traditional Lasat bo-rifle in firing configuration

Unique striping; no two Lasat are the same

GARAZEB "ZEB" ORRELIOS

A hulking Lasat, Zeb is the muscle of the Spectres and not one to keep his temper under control or his opinions hidden. His homeworld was razed by the Empire, so he fights for all Lasats when he bashes stormtroopers.

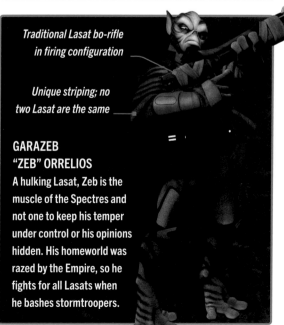

THE *GHOST*

The ragtag nature of the growing Rebellion means that a seemingly simple VCX-100 freighter can become a military command vessel and a crucial component of a galactic revolution. The *Ghost* superficially looks like a typical civilian craft, but it is loaded with modifications that make it essential to the rebel efforts in the Lothal sector. The heart of the *Ghost* is its pilot, Hera Syndulla, who rises in the rebel ranks to become a general.

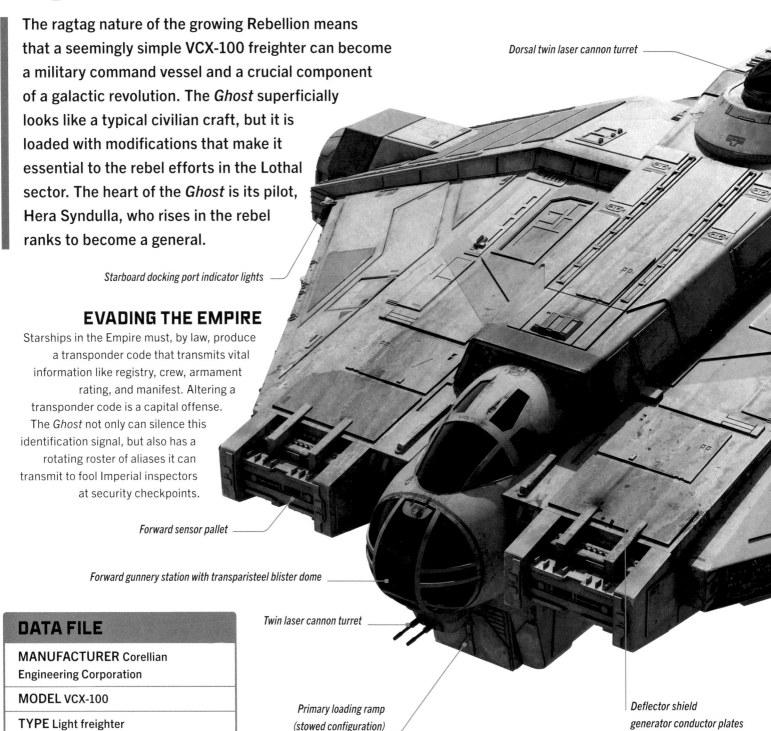

Dorsal twin laser cannon turret

Starboard docking port indicator lights

EVADING THE EMPIRE

Starships in the Empire must, by law, produce a transponder code that transmits vital information like registry, crew, armament rating, and manifest. Altering a transponder code is a capital offense. The *Ghost* not only can silence this identification signal, but also has a rotating roster of aliases it can transmit to fool Imperial inspectors at security checkpoints.

Forward sensor pallet

Forward gunnery station with transparisteel blister dome

DATA FILE

MANUFACTURER Corellian Engineering Corporation	
MODEL VCX-100	
TYPE Light freighter	
DIMENSIONS Length: 43.70 m (143 ft 4 in); width: 13.26 m (43 ft 6 in); height: 33.84 m (111 ft)	
WEAPONS 1 twin laser cannon; 2 laser cannon turrets	
AFFILIATION Rebel Alliance	

Twin laser cannon turret

Primary loading ramp (stowed configuration)

Deflector shield generator conductor plates

THERE'S A LOT YOU DON'T KNOW ABOUT MY SHIP."

– HERA SYNDULLA

Auxiliary craft stow here (currently not docked)

Ion engine
nacelle

Standard docking ring with modular adaptors

Port docking
indicator lights

CAPTAIN OF THE *GHOST*

Since her childhood growing up on Ryloth, Hera Syndulla has dreamed of flight, inspired by the gunship and starfighter pilots of the Galactic Republic. She cut her piloting teeth on a YT-209 freighter before becoming smitten with the capabilities of a VCX-100. Over the years, the *Ghost* has become more than a ship: it is a home for Hera and her found family, the Spectres.

PHANTOM II

Replacing the original *Phantom* is an extensively modified *Sheathipede*-class shuttle, a relic from the Clone Wars salvaged from the planet Agamar. With a greater operational range than its predecessor, the *Phantom II* is equipped with a hyperdrive and astromech socket typically occupied by C1-10P. The *Phantom II* has a livery that befits its new allegiance, designed and painted by Sabine Wren.

PHANTOM

One of the *Ghost*'s surprises is an auxiliary craft stowed in its aft hull. This swift shuttle is modified to increase its performance and firepower, achieving starfighter-level capabilities in terms of maneuverability and combat effectiveness. The *Phantom* is most often deployed as a support or landing craft, as it lacks a hyperdrive. This ship is lost over the planet Yarma.

Articulated
stabilization foil

Heavy laser cannons

Power and data
utility conduit

Forward laser cannon pod

CHAPTER 4

THE CRIMINAL UNDERWORLD

As Imperial rule enriches many legitimate businesses through partnerships that benefit both, the less-than-legal enterprises found across the galaxy also thrive. The criminal underworld, in the cynical view, exists to give the people what they want or need, no matter how illicit, dangerous, or vile. In these dark times, such needs persist and grow, and crime flourishes despite the vaunted efforts of the Empire to enforce law and order.

CRIMINAL SYNDICATES

It is no small irony that an Empire so loudly committed to lawful order results in an increase of crime on a galactic scale. In the time of Imperial rule, five criminal syndicates rise to prominence, governing carefully defined territories and fields of business while maintaining a tense yet honored pact of noncompetition.

Imperial security restrictions have made once commonplace items like medicine and fuel into hard-to-find goods, as legal tariffs and other restrictions price them beyond the range of law-abiding citizens. The wealthy continue to have access to such products while paying a barely felt premium. As basic needs remain unmet, the underworld, as always, is there to fill the gaps.

CRYMORAH

Most secretive of the five syndicates is the Crymorah, an ancient organization situated in the heart of the galaxy. The Crymorah lends its structure to the larger criminal underworld, as it, too, is made up of five families—the Rang Clan, the Wandering Star, the Droid Gotra, the Baldamiro Family, and envoys of the Hutts.

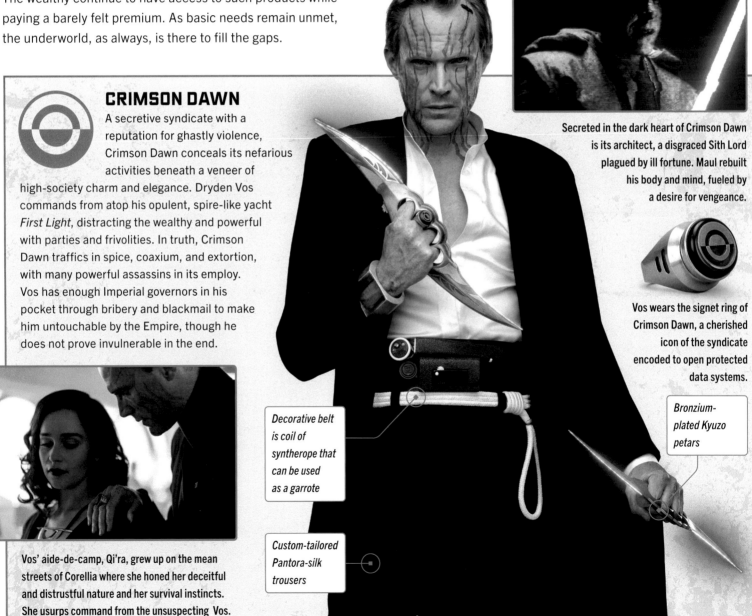

CRIMSON DAWN

A secretive syndicate with a reputation for ghastly violence, Crimson Dawn conceals its nefarious activities beneath a veneer of high-society charm and elegance. Dryden Vos commands from atop his opulent, spire-like yacht *First Light*, distracting the wealthy and powerful with parties and frivolities. In truth, Crimson Dawn traffics in spice, coaxium, and extortion, with many powerful assassins in its employ. Vos has enough Imperial governors in his pocket through bribery and blackmail to make him untouchable by the Empire, though he does not prove invulnerable in the end.

Secreted in the dark heart of Crimson Dawn is its architect, a disgraced Sith Lord plagued by ill fortune. Maul rebuilt his body and mind, fueled by a desire for vengeance.

Vos wears the signet ring of Crimson Dawn, a cherished icon of the syndicate encoded to open protected data systems.

Bronzium-plated Kyuzo petars

Decorative belt is coil of syntherope that can be used as a garrote

Custom-tailored Pantora-silk trousers

Vos' aide-de-camp, Qi'ra, grew up on the mean streets of Corellia where she honed her deceitful and distrustful nature and her survival instincts. She usurps command from the unsuspecting Vos.

PYKES

The Pykes of Oba Diah derive their power from their control of the spice mines of Kessel, an exclusive arrangement reached with the monarch of that despoiled world. The valuable mineral has legitimate medicinal applications, but it can also be refined into strains of narcotics that have become the blight of many worlds.

The strip-mined hemisphere of Kessel is an ecological nightmare, with prison labor enduring the toxic conditions to extract spice or coaxium from the planet's crust.

Mechno-arm replacing limb lost in mining mishap

Decrepit filtration gear to eliminate airborne toxins

Array of caretaker access keys

BLACK SUN

Formerly based on Mustafar, Black Sun is a consortium of varied businesses masterminded by Falleen overlords in the Outer Rim Territories. They control several major shipping routes through the employ of legitimate transport corporations as a front. During the Clone Wars they served Maul as a major backer of the Shadow Collective, the ad-hoc criminal enterprise that precipitated his involvement in Crimson Dawn.

Quilted armor with duraweave fiber

Captain of the Guard uniform

Identity-concealing foot soldier helmet

HUTT CARTEL

The Hutts have long ruled a sizable patch of space in the eastern Outer Rim, dominating a wide array of criminal ventures. The Hutts' inroads with the Crymorah Syndicate have brought Outer Rim vices deep into the heart of the Core Worlds. The leader of the Hutt Cartel, Jabba Desilijic Tiure, keeps himself separated from the centers of power on Coruscant or Nal Hutta by maintaining his headquarters on an obscure desert planet, Tatooine.

Succulent gorg snack

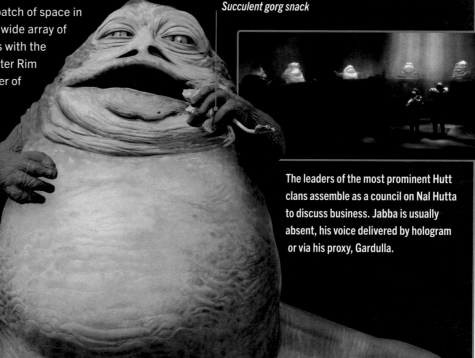

Jabba the Hutt relishes the comforts of power and forces those seeking audience with him to venture to his remote world.

The leaders of the most prominent Hutt clans assemble as a council on Nal Hutta to discuss business. Jabba is usually absent, his voice delivered by hologram or via his proxy, Gardulla.

QI'RA ASCENDANT

Qi'ra has quietly observed the nature of power in the underworld, first under the rule of Lady Proxima and the White Worms of Corellia. She demonstrates enough talent that Proxima opts not to kill her for her botched attempt at escape; instead, Qi'ra is traded to Crimson Dawn. Qi'ra maneuvers her way into an essential leadership position, a heartbeat away from commanding the syndicate.

GALACTIC CRIMINALS

Aside from the overarching criminal syndicates, the underworld of the galaxy offers a colorful gallery of smaller organizations and independent operators willing to bend Imperial law in exchange for hard credits. Mercenaries can readily find work in the Outer Rim and Hutt Space if they're not fazed by the lethality of the criminal trade. Crime families often rely on such hired guns if direct connections to their ranks would create too many complications.

As the threat of rebellion grows within the Empire, so, too, does pressure on smaller criminal enterprises. After a particularly galling theft of Imperial credits at Aldhani, an emergency session of the Senate ratifies the Public Order Resentencing Directive, a package of punitive measures that amplifies sentences and fines for a wide array of crimes. Those powerful enough to be well-placed within syndicates are insulated from such security measures. Other less influential criminals begin to view the rebellion with greater sympathy. They dare to take a side in the conflict, working discreetly to hasten the Empire's fall.

AZMORIGAN

A greedy and slovenly Jablogian, Azmorigan carves a disreputable niche in the shadows of Hutt Space, becoming successful enough to further inflate his outsized ego. He later goes on to steal from Imperial transports, despite claims of being apolitical.

IG-RM bodyguard droid

Coin pouch with forged currency

THE BROKEN HORN

Though self-described as a syndicate, the Broken Horn is a small operation focused primarily on the underworld of Lothal. Untrusting subordinates, Cikatro Vizago mostly works alone, with only a cadre of bodyguard droids in his employ.

Cranial comms implant in the base of Nokru's skull

DAIYU

A kaleidoscopic cacophony of squalor, decadence, garish lights, and shadow, Daiyu is a mostly lawless world awash in sleaze and vice. Urban sprawl covers most of Daiyu's surface, and criminals pack the alleyways and thoroughfares, offering illicit market goods in the open. Bounty hunters prowl the markets in search of profitable tips, as the petty thieves that abound aren't worth their time. Daiyu is a place where people come to disappear.

THE BLACK MASK

Based out of Daiyu City, Vect Nokru leads a gang of mercenaries called the Black Mask, which includes Ayo Bons and Vidara Jurness.

WHITE WORMS

The White Worms are criminal leaders that exploit abandoned youths in the slums of Corellia. The so-called scrumrats act as pickpockets and thieves, bringing back goods to the sewer-dwelling Grindalids in exchange for favor, food, and shelter.

Lady Proxima, elder Grindalid

WANTED BY LAW

GRINI MILLEGI
Grini Millegi is a hulking Dowutin gambler who uses his muscle to ensure the riot races of the Safa Toma Speedway come out in his favor.

HAXION BROOD
Led by the vengeful Sorc Tormo, the Haxion Brood is a deadly bounty hunters syndicate for hire with a vendetta against Jedi Cal Kestis.

VANGUARD AXIS
An offshoot of the Droid Gotra crime family, the all-droid Axis enforcers deal primarily in stolen identicodes and other illicit data.

ROLAND DURAN
The son of a prominent crime lord, Roland Duran hopes to carve out his own dominance in the spice trade of Ord Mantell.

CID
An aged Trandoshan, Cid is a trader who worked both sides of the Clone Wars to great profit. More valuable than credits is her sprawling network of contacts, and her greatest skill is as a connector.

Vestigial plume rachis

"ISN'T THAT PART OF ORD MANTELL A LITTLE... SEEDY?"
- TRACE MARTEZ

ORD MANTELL
Founded as an ordnance/regional depot during the Old Republic by Corellian colonists, Ord Mantell is an ancient trading port with a lively blend of numerous cultures. The sprawl of Ord Mantell City, the capital, is a popular smugglers' haven, as the Empire expends little effort in maintaining a permanent presence there.

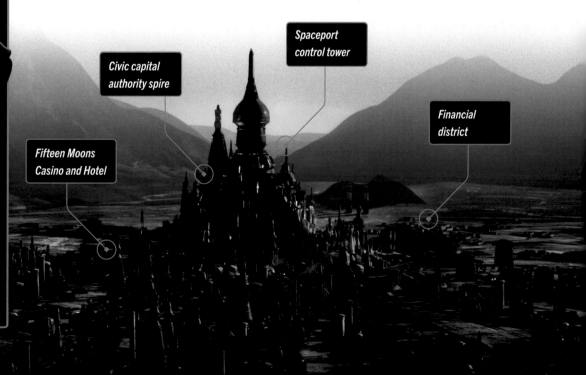

Civic capital authority spire

Spaceport control tower

Financial district

Fifteen Moons Casino and Hotel

SMUGGLERS

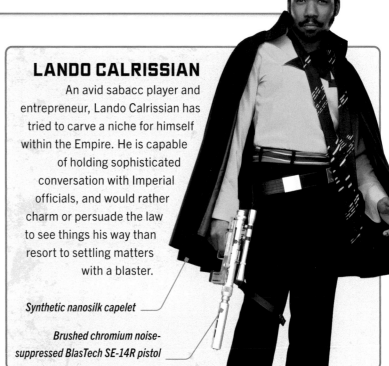

With the nationalization of the Trade Federation in the fallout from the Clone Wars, a huge gulf emerges between the big transportation needs of major multisystem concerns and the small cargo shipments from individual citizens. There are many legitimate reasons to use independent operators. Terms may be pricey, but are often negotiable. A lack of bureaucracy and record-keeping is ideal for clients seeking discretion. But what if the cargo is of dubious legality or outright contraband? These goods necessitate the hiring of smugglers.

With Imperial prohibitions on the rise and the sentences for breaking said prohibitions getting steeper by the day, the smuggling trade flourishes under the Empire. As risks rise, so do rewards for the capable smuggler. The Rebellion has come to rely on smugglers for transport of goods and personnel, but the independent cargo ship operators are a notoriously apolitical lot. They don't seek revolution: they seek to exploit the cracks in unfair systems and profit where they can. The nature of the Empire and its goal of total domination will severely test this cynicism.

LANDO CALRISSIAN

An avid sabacc player and entrepreneur, Lando Calrissian has tried to carve a niche for himself within the Empire. He is capable of holding sophisticated conversation with Imperial officials, and would rather charm or persuade the law to see things his way than resort to settling matters with a blaster.

Synthetic nanosilk capelet

Brushed chromium noise-suppressed BlasTech SE-14R pistol

HONDO OHNAKA

A swashbuckling Weequay pirate from Sriluur whose reputation pales in comparison to his estimation of what it should be, Hondo Ohnaka has been plying the spacelanes as a pirate and smuggler since the Clone Wars. His fortunes are as unpredictable as his loyalty.

— *Keratin jawline growths typical of aging Weequays*

SANA STARROS

Captain of the *Volt Cobra*, Sana Starros has affiliated herself with various criminal organizations and shady enterprises while making a living on the fringe. She comes from a long line of independent-minded rulebreakers. Sana has worked with a range of scoundrels, including Lando Calrissian, Chelli Aphra, and Han Solo—even posing as Solo's wife to pull off a scam.

Scopeless SE-14R to facilitate drawing quickly

LOBOT

Lobot is a close friend of Lando Calrissian and his partner in many capers across the galaxy. He uses his BioTech AJ^6 cerebral augs to great effect in bypassing security systems. One grueling use to save Lando's life aboard Emperor Palpatine's yacht the *Imperialis* deeply affected Lobot's once colorful personality, a situation Calrissian has sworn to correct.

PHEE GENOA

A treasure hunter and adventure-seeker, Phee Genoa considers herself to be "a liberator of ancient wonders" rather than a trader in illegally obtained antiquities. By her reasoning, most ancient wares shouldn't reside in private collections, and absconding with them in order to return them to those whose cultures they belong to is a way of balancing out the scales.

HAN SOLO

Unlike many smugglers, Han Solo has firsthand experience under the Imperial banner. Desperate to leave an impoverished life committing crimes on Corellia, he signs up for the Academy. Despite exceptional skills, his recklessness gets him drummed out of pilot service and he later serves as an infantryman slogging through the trenches of Mimban. Solo's true return to lawbreaking follows his joining Tobias Beckett's crew, an entanglement with Crimson Dawn, and seeing Lando Calrissian's *Millennium Falcon* for the first time. His affiliation with the Alliance comes later.

CHEWIE AND HAN

A lifelong friendship forms between Han and Chewbacca following their escape from an Imperial stockade. The two come to rely on each other in a partnership that spans numerous successes and setbacks. A superb mechanic, Chewie serves as Han's conscience and is pivotal to steering Han to the Rebellion.

DATA FILE

SUBJECT	Han Solo
HOMEWORLD	Corellia
SPECIES	Human
AFFILIATION	Formerly White Worms; formerly Imperial; independent
HEIGHT	1.83 m (6 ft)
AGE	22 (10 BBY)

Nerf-leather jacket with hidden interior pockets

BlasTech universal DL-series power ammunition pack

BLASTECH DL-44 HEAVY BLASTER PISTOL

Low-slung cutaway quick-draw holster

Double buckle with thigh holster extension

FACT FILE

While smugglers prize independence, many are in debt to guilds or mobsters who help cover their starship operating expenses.

The Corporate Sector Authority in particular has a poor view of independent spacers, waging a public relations campaign against them.

MILLENNIUM FALCON

Without a dedicated support fleet to move goods and people across the galaxy, the early Rebellion relies on independent operators long used to working in the shadowy areas of Imperial shipping regulations. All manner of rogues, including smugglers and pirates, sign up for a price. The crew of the *Millennium Falcon* becomes one of the most famous examples. In fact, the battered YT-1300 light freighter has flown beyond its humble origins and into galactic history.

Starboard airlock docking collar

Passage tube from cockpit to ring corridor

Cockpit module bearing identification markings

KapriCorp acceleration compensator

Now superfluous maintenance access portal

SCOUNDRELS IN FLIGHT

The most well-known *Falcon* crew members, Han Solo and Chewbacca, each have their own reasons to despise the Empire, though they attempt to remain apolitical in their smuggling career. One of their first heists—a trove of coaxium—inadvertently ends up funding a rebel movement when they are intercepted by Enfys Nest and her gang of Cloud-Riders.

Tractor beam subsystems

Gelieg C-beam lamp housing

Forward cargo-handling mandible

"SHE MAY NOT LOOK LIKE MUCH, BUT SHE'S GOT IT WHERE IT COUNTS..."
– HAN SOLO

EVOLVING DESIGN

The secret to the *Falcon*'s successes and failures is that it is full of surprises, due to a chaotic patchwork of repairs and modifications woven throughout the ship. Its hyperdrive, sublight systems, lift-mass ratio, armament rating, and hull plating are well beyond legal limits, but are concealed beneath a patina of grime, a maze of welded innards, and a forest of tangled wiring.

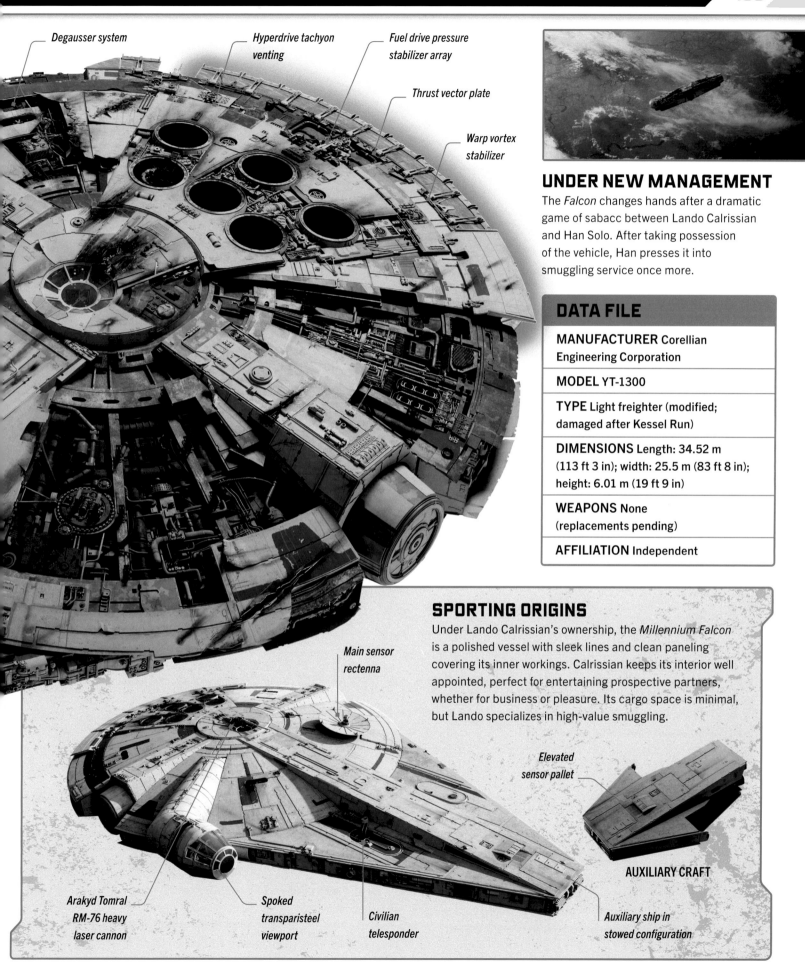

Degausser system

Hyperdrive tachyon venting

Fuel drive pressure stabilizer array

Thrust vector plate

Warp vortex stabilizer

UNDER NEW MANAGEMENT

The *Falcon* changes hands after a dramatic game of sabacc between Lando Calrissian and Han Solo. After taking possession of the vehicle, Han presses it into smuggling service once more.

DATA FILE

MANUFACTURER Corellian Engineering Corporation

MODEL YT-1300

TYPE Light freighter (modified; damaged after Kessel Run)

DIMENSIONS Length: 34.52 m (113 ft 3 in); width: 25.5 m (83 ft 8 in); height: 6.01 m (19 ft 9 in)

WEAPONS None (replacements pending)

AFFILIATION Independent

SPORTING ORIGINS

Under Lando Calrissian's ownership, the *Millennium Falcon* is a polished vessel with sleek lines and clean paneling covering its inner workings. Calrissian keeps its interior well appointed, perfect for entertaining prospective partners, whether for business or pleasure. Its cargo space is minimal, but Lando specializes in high-value smuggling.

Main sensor rectenna

Elevated sensor pallet

AUXILIARY CRAFT

Arakyd Tomral RM-76 heavy laser cannon

Spoked transparisteel viewport

Civilian telesponder

Auxiliary ship in stowed configuration

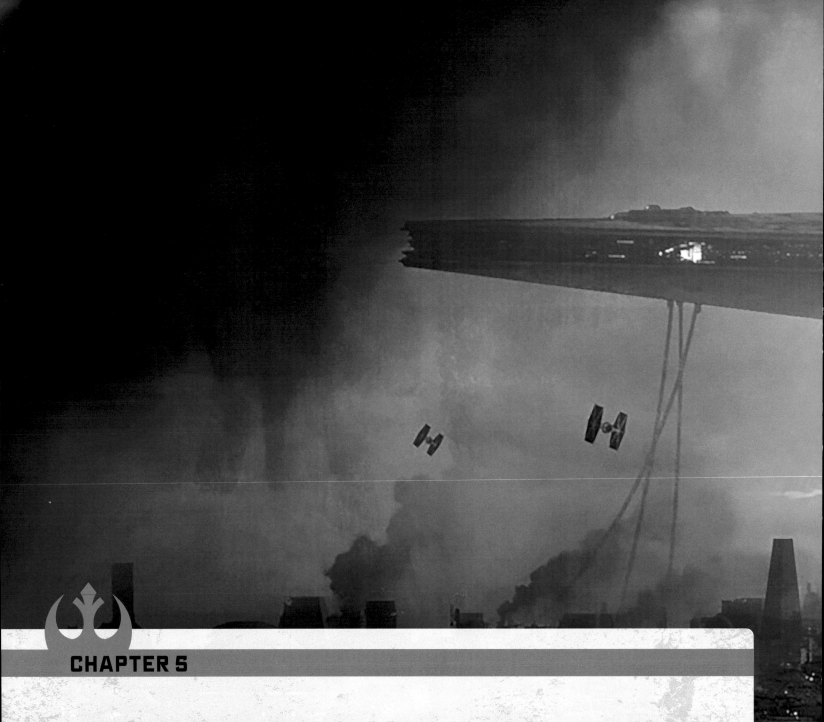

CHAPTER 5

INSTRUMENTS OF THE EMPIRE

The icons of the Empire are unmistakable: enormous arrowhead-shaped warships, swarming flat-winged starfighters, lumbering mechanical walkers, and the stark white armor of endless armies. These weapons of oppression are carefully engineered to strike terror into the hearts of would-be rebels, so the Empire wins by the threat of force alone.

IMPERIAL DESTROYERS

The Clone Wars inspired a rush of innovation in capital ship design, a realm that had not required any change in centuries of peace. A veritable arms race between Separatist and Republic weapons development enriched industrialists who straddled both sides, feigning neutrality while profiting immensely. A victor in this race is Kuat Drive Yards, a factory world ruled by traditionalist aristocrats who are proud to fully embrace the Imperial vision of galactic dominance through unchallenged capital ship power.

Star Destroyer bridges of all subsequent models follow the mold of the *Venator*-class from the Clone Wars. Within the bridge tower, pit crews work beneath an elevated walkway from which the command staff oversee operations.

DATA FILE

MANUFACTURER Kuat Drive Yards

MODEL *Imperial I*-class

TYPE Star Destroyer

DIMENSIONS Length: 1,600.52 m (5,251 ft 1 in); width: 985.17 m (3,232 ft 2 in); height: 455.40 m (1,461 ft 3 in)

WEAPONS 60 Taim & Bak XX-9 heavy turbolaser batteries; 60 Borstel NK-7 ion cannons; 10 Phylon Q7 tractor beam projectors

AFFILIATION Galactic Empire

Medical substation (typical)

Officers' recreation section (typical)

Deflector shield projection port (typical)

High-frequency communication transmission station

Sensor pallet (typical)

Ventral tractor beam projector

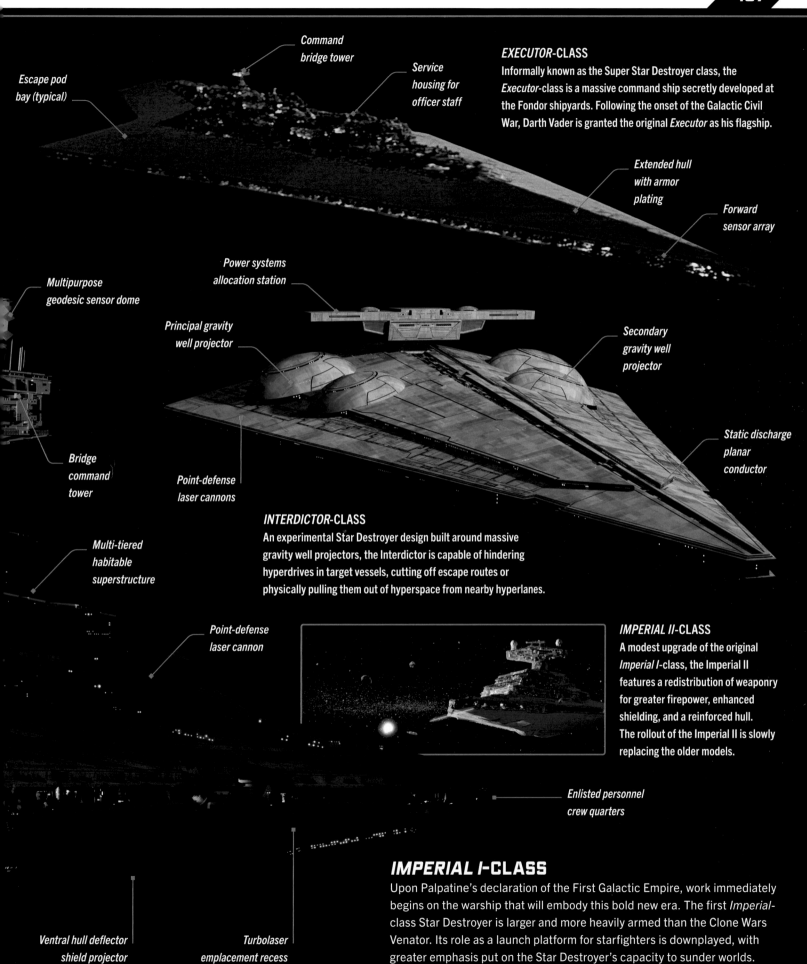

Escape pod
bay (typical)

Command
bridge tower

Service
housing for
officer staff

EXECUTOR-CLASS
Informally known as the Super Star Destroyer class, the *Executor*-class is a massive command ship secretly developed at the Fondor shipyards. Following the onset of the Galactic Civil War, Darth Vader is granted the original *Executor* as his flagship.

Extended hull
with armor
plating

Forward
sensor array

Multipurpose
geodesic sensor dome

Power systems
allocation station

Principal gravity
well projector

Secondary
gravity well
projector

Bridge
command
tower

Point-defense
laser cannons

Static discharge
planar
conductor

Multi-tiered
habitable
superstructure

INTERDICTOR-CLASS
An experimental Star Destroyer design built around massive gravity well projectors, the Interdictor is capable of hindering hyperdrives in target vessels, cutting off escape routes or physically pulling them out of hyperspace from nearby hyperlanes.

Point-defense
laser cannon

IMPERIAL II-CLASS
A modest upgrade of the original *Imperial I*-class, the Imperial II features a redistribution of weaponry for greater firepower, enhanced shielding, and a reinforced hull. The rollout of the Imperial II is slowly replacing the older models.

Enlisted personnel
crew quarters

IMPERIAL I-CLASS
Upon Palpatine's declaration of the First Galactic Empire, work immediately begins on the warship that will embody this bold new era. The first *Imperial*-class Star Destroyer is larger and more heavily armed than the Clone Wars Venator. Its role as a launch platform for starfighters is downplayed, with greater emphasis put on the Star Destroyer's capacity to sunder worlds.

Ventral hull deflector
shield projector

Turbolaser
emplacement recess

IMPERIAL CRUISERS

The angular, arrowhead silhouette of the Kuat Drive Yards destroyer casts a long shadow on the Imperial fleet, and has become an icon of galactic naval power. Other more specialized vessels mimic this look, as it so easily inspires fear. Imperial doctrine favors the construction of ever-larger warships, but the practicality of ruling over a varied galaxy requires tailored craft for specific applications. Nonetheless, unifying these ships with a similar aesthetic helps convey an essential message of Imperial rule: there is nowhere to hide.

DATA FILE

MANUFACTURER Kuat Drive Yards

MODEL *Cantwell*-class Arrestor

TYPE Patrol and detainment cruiser

DIMENSIONS Length: 1,363.13 m (4,472 ft 3 in); width: 667.42 m (2,189 ft 8 in); height: 229.78 m (753 ft 11 in)

WEAPONS Triple tractor beam array; three heavy turbolaser turrets; two ion cannon turrets

AFFILIATION Galactic Empire

"WE COULD USE THE PRACTICE. PREPARE FOR BOARDING AND INSPECTION, HAULCRAFT."

– CAPTAIN ELK

Primary tractor beam projector on articulated mount

Positioning systems

Dedicated tractor power trunk connected directly to reactor

Parabolic amplifier

IMPERIAL LIGHT CARRIER

The *Quasar Fire*-class cruiser-carrier can rapidly launch up to eight TIE squadrons, comprising 96 fighters. Its cavernous holds carry fully stocked repair and resupply bays, technical crews, and maintenance droids to rival the personnel and equipment of planetary launch bases. The ship itself is well armed and armored.

Underslung bridge/ command deck

Armored deck covers launch bays

Budgetary frugality and a desire to enshrine the dominance of larger craft in the Imperial Navy means that the bulk of the starfighter designs lack hyperdrive

CANTWELL-CLASS CRUISER

Named for famed starship designer Walex Cantwell Blissex I, the Arrestor cruiser is a specialized starship for enforcing security along Imperial spacelanes. This angular craft is built around massive tractor beam projectors that can pinpoint and reel suspect starships into its holding bays or keep them immobilized until other ships arrive.

Sensor masts scrutinize target conditions

Command bridge

Office spaces for customs and border control personnel

Launch and holding bay

Emphasis on a singular function creates exploitable weaknesses, as Luthen Rael proves in his escape from an Arrestor above Segra Milo. Sensor countermeasures deceive the Arrestor's crew, and destructive chaff shred its tractor beam projectors, using the cruiser's own tractor beam against it.

Portside secondary tractor beam projector

Reinforced hull reduces shear forces

CLASS FOUR CONTAINER TRANSPORTS

KDY Class Four transports avoid the storage limitations of container ships past by doing away with enclosed bays and instead arrange standardized containers in a tractor field grid, essentially becoming a super tug. While this makes cargo more vulnerable to external attack, these ships are rarely unescorted.

Command bridge

Turbolaser turret for defense

Reinforced hull

Tractor projector systems

Inertial guidance systems

A grid of 210 cargo modules is the typical standard yield for a Class Four transport. Dedicated inventory droids aboard keep track of contents, arranging the containers for maximum efficiency.

Forward deflector shield projector

IMPERIAL TRANSPORTS

While massive warships get the glory in Imperial fleet action, stalwart transport craft keep those larger ships supplied with fuel, munitions, parts, and personnel, and also ferry important Imperial leaders to their destinations. Transport pilots perform this thankless and tireless work to keep the Imperial military machine functioning, and many noteworthy defections to the Rebellion have come from their ranks.

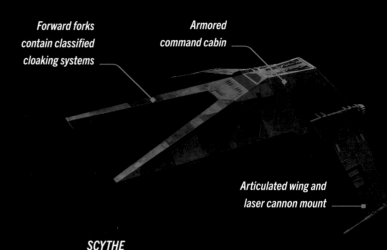

Forward forks contain classified cloaking systems

Armored command cabin

Articulated wing and laser cannon mount

SCYTHE

The command ship of the Inquisitorius, the *Scythe* is a *Phi*-class shuttle with an exceedingly efficient hyperdrive for a ship of this compact size. It often transports the Grand Inquisitor.

Hyperdrive motivator and related subsystems

Ion turbine engine

Turbine intake and ramscoop

Twin laser cannon turret

Bridge viewport

Outer docking superstructure

DATA FILE

MANUFACTURER Corellian Engineering Corporation

MODEL *Gozanti*-class

TYPE Transport and carrier

DIMENSIONS Length: 62.75 m (205 ft 11 in); width: 31.45 m (103 ft 2 in); height: 13.05 m (42 ft 10 in)

WEAPONS Twin laser cannon turret; heavy laser cannon turret

AFFILIATION Galactic Empire

GOZANTI-CLASS

A repurposing of a popular civilian design, the Empire's edition of the Gozanti cruiser is also known as an Imperial freighter or an Imperial assault carrier, depending on its configuration. The ship stays true to Corellian design principals and is extensively modular.

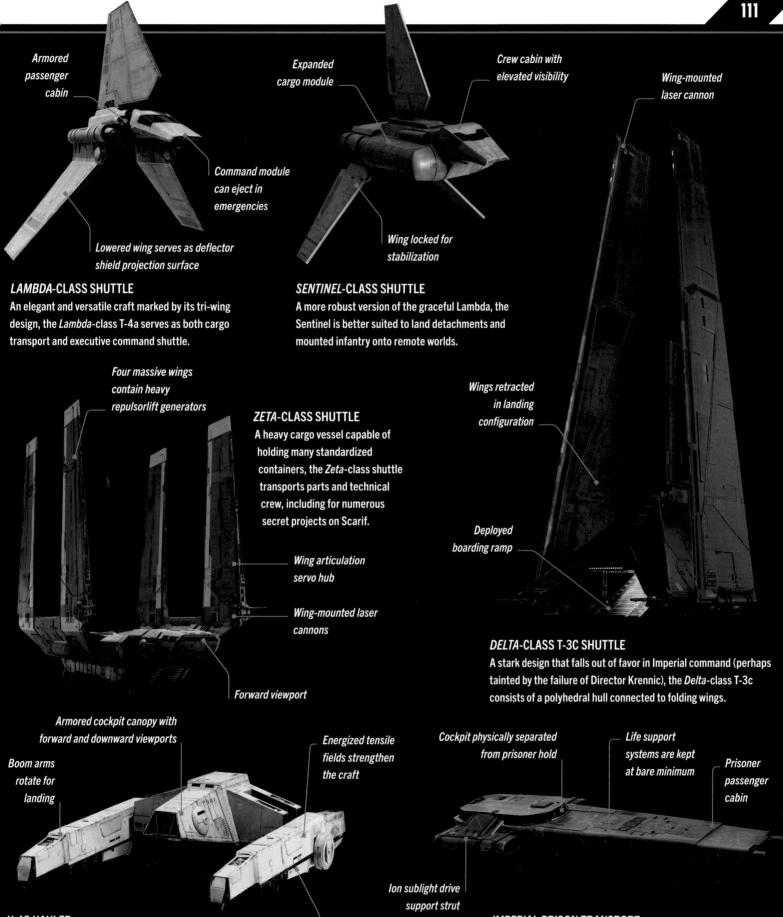

Armored passenger cabin

Command module can eject in emergencies

Lowered wing serves as deflector shield projection surface

LAMBDA-CLASS SHUTTLE

An elegant and versatile craft marked by its tri-wing design, the *Lambda*-class T-4a serves as both cargo transport and executive command shuttle.

Expanded cargo module

Crew cabin with elevated visibility

Wing locked for stabilization

SENTINEL-CLASS SHUTTLE

A more robust version of the graceful Lambda, the Sentinel is better suited to land detachments and mounted infantry onto remote worlds.

Wing-mounted laser cannon

Four massive wings contain heavy repulsorlift generators

Wings retracted in landing configuration

ZETA-CLASS SHUTTLE

A heavy cargo vessel capable of holding many standardized containers, the *Zeta*-class shuttle transports parts and technical crew, including for numerous secret projects on Scarif.

Wing articulation servo hub

Wing-mounted laser cannons

Forward viewport

Deployed boarding ramp

DELTA-CLASS T-3C SHUTTLE

A stark design that falls out of favor in Imperial command (perhaps tainted by the failure of Director Krennic), the *Delta*-class T-3c consists of a polyhedral hull connected to folding wings.

Armored cockpit canopy with forward and downward viewports

Boom arms rotate for landing

Energized tensile fields strengthen the craft

Cockpit physically separated from prisoner hold

Life support systems are kept at bare minimum

Prisoner passenger cabin

Ion sublight drive support strut

Heavy repulsors provide atmospheric lift

Y-45 HAULER

An older Imperial design for the swift battlefield deployment of armored walkers, the AT-hauler has heavy cargo-lifting arms with retractable winching assembly.

IMPERIAL PRISON TRANSPORT

Found ferrying prisoners to worlds like Narkina 5, the Imperial Prison Transport (or IPT) is a repurposing of a troop transport vessel with all comforts stripped out and new restraints added.

TIE FIGHTERS

Though the sheer imposing size of the Imperial Star Destroyer makes it the preferred symbol of the navy, the ubiquitous TIE fighter is an unmistakable contender. A single TIE fighter is an ominous portent, not for its own destructive capability, but for what it heralds: TIEs have limited operational range, so the presence of one indicates an Imperial support system nearby.

The TIE silhouette is unmistakable, carried across a whole series of variants and specialized models. It is easily recognized by its rounded hull and its planar solar gather panels. The twin ion engines that give the series its name also bestow each model a distinct shriek as it soars by. The characteristic swarm tactics used by TIE fighter pilots also point to the TIE's vulnerabilities. On their own, these mass-produced ships with budget-conscience shortcomings can be outmaneuvered by skilled rebel pilots.

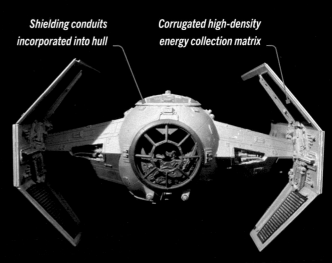

Shielding conduits incorporated into hull

Corrugated high-density energy collection matrix

TIE ADVANCED x1

Darth Vader supplied Sienar Fleet Systems with exacting specifications for a starfighter that would become the prototype x1, notable for its enlarged frame, longer panels, and integrated hyperdrive system.

DATA FILE

MANUFACTURER Sienar Fleet Systems	
MODEL TIE/ln	
TYPE Space superiority starfighter	
DIMENSIONS Length: 7.2 m (23 ft 8 in); width: 6.7 m (22 ft); height: 8.8 m (28 ft 11 in)	
WEAPONS Twin laser cannons	
AFFILIATION Galactic Empire	

TIE FIGHTER

Designated the TIE/ln space superiority starfighter, this is the baseline model that forms the vast bulk of Imperial starfighter corps. TIEs lack hyperdrives, so they rely on carrier ships for transportation to a battlefield beyond the range of the location of their base. These vessels fly in dense wing maneuvers to cover their lack of deflector shields.

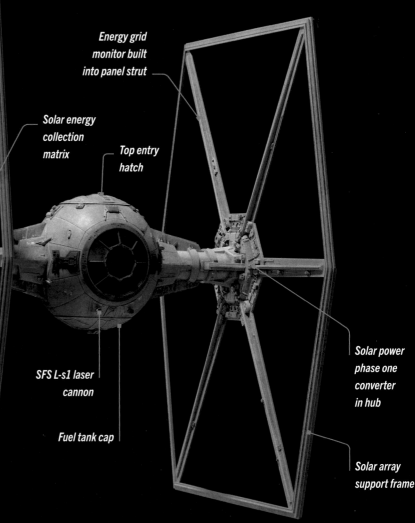

Energy grid monitor built into panel strut

Solar energy collection matrix

Top entry hatch

SFS L-s1 laser cannon

Fuel tank cap

Solar power phase one converter in hub

Solar array support frame

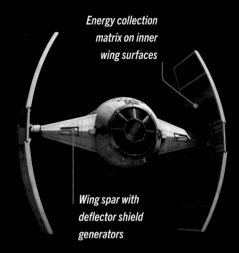

Energy collection matrix on inner wing surfaces

Wing spar with deflector shield generators

TIE ADVANCED v1

Taking design cues from Vader's x1 specs, the Advanced v1 is an elite model used by the Inquisitorius. The ship's collapsible wings minimize its hangar footprint.

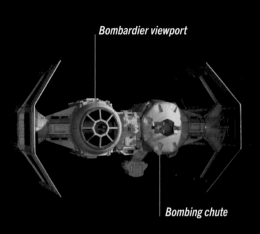

Bombardier viewport

Bombing chute

TIE BOMBER

The cylindrical portside hull of the double-bodied TIE/sa bomber serves as its bomb bay, carrying a wide variety of explosive ordnance.

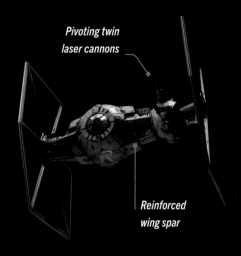

Pivoting twin laser cannons

Reinforced wing spar

TIE BRUTE

A heavy-duty combat fighter, the TIE/rb has a reinforced hull, a remote-operated artillery turret, and a droid intelligence offering the pilot in-flight support.

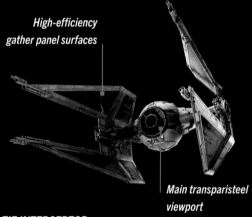

High-efficiency gather panel surfaces

Main transparisteel viewport

TIE INTERCEPTOR

The high-speed successor to the x1 prototype, the TIE/in interceptor has dagger-shaped wings that increase pilot visibility and provide incredible speed and maneuverability.

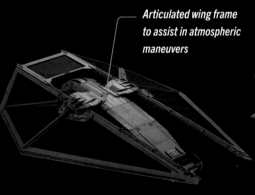

Articulated wing frame to assist in atmospheric maneuvers

TIE REAPER

An attack lander designed to ferry troops to battlefields, such as squads of elite death troopers, the reaper has thick armor and strong deflector shields.

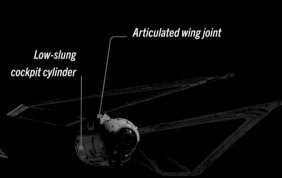

Articulated wing joint

Low-slung cockpit cylinder

TIE STRIKER

An experimental fighter for defending planetary bases, the TIE/sk x1 is a high-atmosphere fighter streamlined for aerial combat yet capable of low orbit.

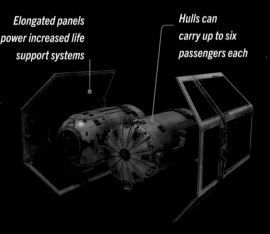

Class 2 hyperdrive equipped

Elongated panels power increased life support systems

Hulls can carry up to six passengers each

TIE DEFENDER

The ultimate cutting-edge model, the TIE/d defender is championed by Grand Admiral Thrawn to be the answer to rebel starfighter superiority.

TIE BOARDING CRAFT

A TIE/sa variant, the boarding craft replaces the bomber's ordnance bay with a docking-hatch-equipped passenger bay that can carry a squad of stormtroopers.

MINING GUILD TIE FIGHTER

A rare example of Sienar Fleet Systems repurposing a military design for a civilian model, the TIE/mg protects mining guild operations from pirates and claim jumpers (illicit miners).

Black-and-yellow Mining Guild livery

Cutaway wings increase mineral sensor visibility

IMPERIAL WALKERS

The towering epitome of Imperial design philosophy, the armored walker series emphasizes psychological terror over mechanical practicalities. The Clone Wars saw rapid development of walkers, and the corporations aligned with the victorious Republic transformed lessons learned into design innovations for the emerging Imperial Army.

Consolidation of leading industrial firms, directed by high-ranking Imperial officials, ushers in the emergence of Kuat Drive Yards (KDY) as the vanguard not only of capital warship production, but walker production, too. Smaller companies are swallowed whole by KDY, and some competitors are violently taken over. KDY now looms large over walker research, development, and distribution. Imperial generals proudly march into battle ensconced in their enormous mechanical monsters.

AT-AT

Early models of the All Terrain Armored Transport are larger than the final production line as mass and material tolerances are pushed to their limits. The testbed model (retroactively cataloged as the AT-AT/P) proves successful enough to stay in use even after it has been supplanted by improved models.

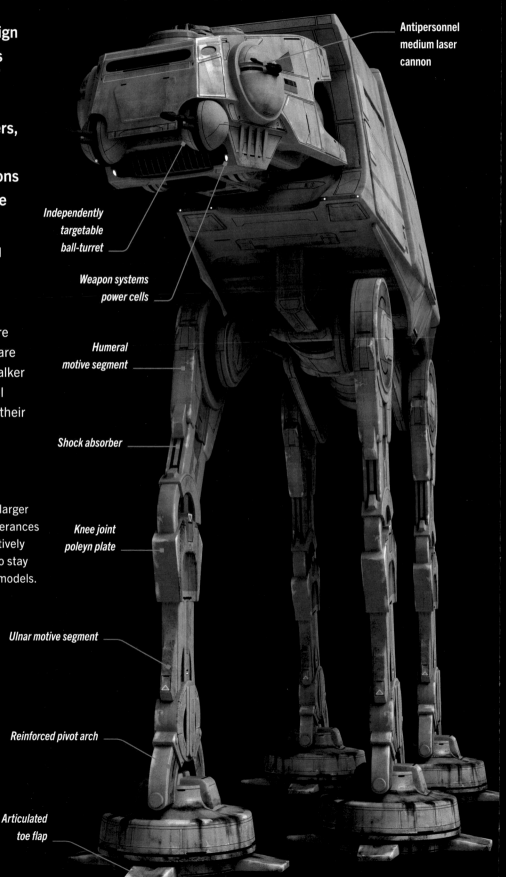

Antipersonnel medium laser cannon

Independently targetable ball-turret

Weapon systems power cells

Humeral motive segment

Shock absorber

Knee joint poleyn plate

Ulnar motive segment

Reinforced pivot arch

Articulated toe flap

DATA FILE

MANUFACTURER Kuat Drive Yards	
MODEL AT-AT/P	
TYPE All Terrain Armored Transport (Prototype)	
DIMENSIONS Length: 31.17 m (102 ft 3 in); width: 12.24 m (40 ft 2 in); height: 26.7 m (87 ft 7 in)	
WEAPONS 2 heavy laser cannon ball-turrets; 2 antipersonnel laser cannons	
AFFILIATION Galactic Empire	

Flashback suppression armor

Modular turbolaser artillery piece

Recoil distributing legs

AT-DT
The All Terrain Defense Turret is a single-pilot mobile artillery platform used for distance strikes in advance of infantry deployment. The AT-DT's open cockpit design means it is best kept far away from close entanglements.

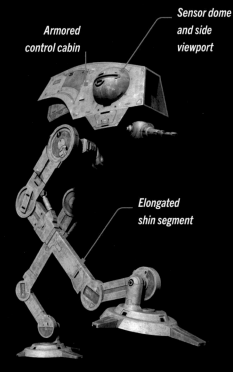

Armored control cabin

Sensor dome and side viewport

Elongated shin segment

AT-DP
The All Terrain Defense Pod is a swift-footed scouting vehicle suitable for urban deployment. These walkers are easier to maneuver through congested streets than other walker models.

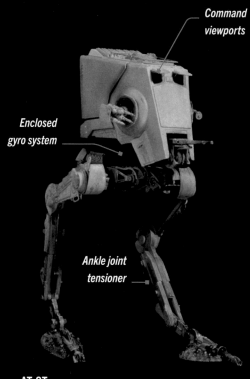

Command viewports

Enclosed gyro system

Ankle joint tensioner

AT-ST
The All Terrain Scout Transport is a recon and patrol vehicle that, when deployed in conjunction with larger AT-ATs, can mop up enemy infantry or intercept would-be saboteurs.

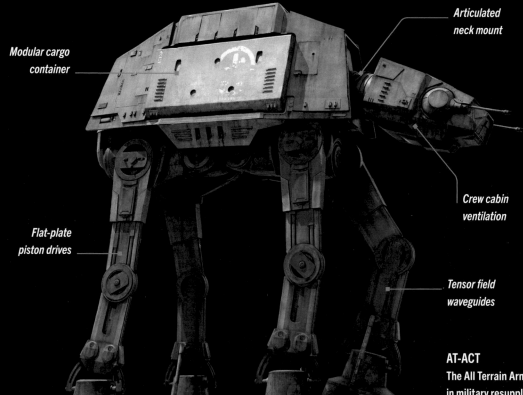

Modular cargo container

Articulated neck mount

Flat-plate piston drives

Crew cabin ventilation

Tensor field waveguides

AT-AC
An early model of the urban suppression walker, the All Terrain Armored Cannon turns a single pilot into a mobile weapons battery. The vehicle has two pivoting double antipersonnel cannons, which extend from an armored control cabin.

AT-ACT
The All Terrain Armored Cargo Transport is a carrier walker used in military resupply convoys. While not intended as a battlefield vehicle, its defensive systems allow it to protect valuable cargo

IMPERIAL SPEEDERS AND GROUND VEHICLES

Control of Imperial territory ultimately comes down to dominance of the very ground of the planets being subjugated. In addition to its armored walking titans, the Empire relies on swift repulsorcraft and other technologies to move its forces quickly across vast expanses of varied terrain. Unlike the ill-equipped rebels, who must modify their vehicles to suit the environment, the Empire can afford a wide array of specialized craft.

"THOSE BIKES ARE FROM THE IMPERIAL FACTORY. I HAVE PEOPLE ON THE INSIDE WHO BUILD THEM TO BREAK."
– RYDER AZADI, FORMER LOTHAL GOVERNOR

Control handle rail slot

Internal gyroscopic stabilizer

BlasTech AX-25 blaster cannon

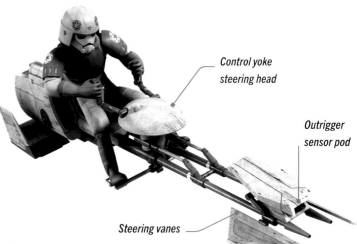

Control yoke steering head

Outrigger sensor pod

Steering vanes

C-PH
While urban patrol is usually left to local police forces, some industrial worlds are valuable enough to attract Imperial military protection. The C-PH is a military police speeder found patrolling near factories on such planets as Corellia and Ferrix.

614-AVA
A venerable speeder bike design with a robust power plant, sturdier driver's seat, and more primitive control yoke than the 74-Z, the Aratech 614-AVA is still in use in the Outer Rim. Its power plant allows an extended operational range.

CONVEYEX
The conveyex is a specialized Imperial transport for moving cargo across frontier planets, necessitating the construction of a dedicated rail line. The conveyex consists of a drive engine, a train of cargo modules, and a stabilizing caboose typically fitted with a laser cannon emplacement. The drive module pulls the train along a heavy chain that fits into the rail design.

Drive-link housing drum

Reinforced chain bar rails

Double medium repeating laser cannons

Hitch joint coupler

Underslung drive module

Magnetic pallet stabilizes inner cargo during orientation changes

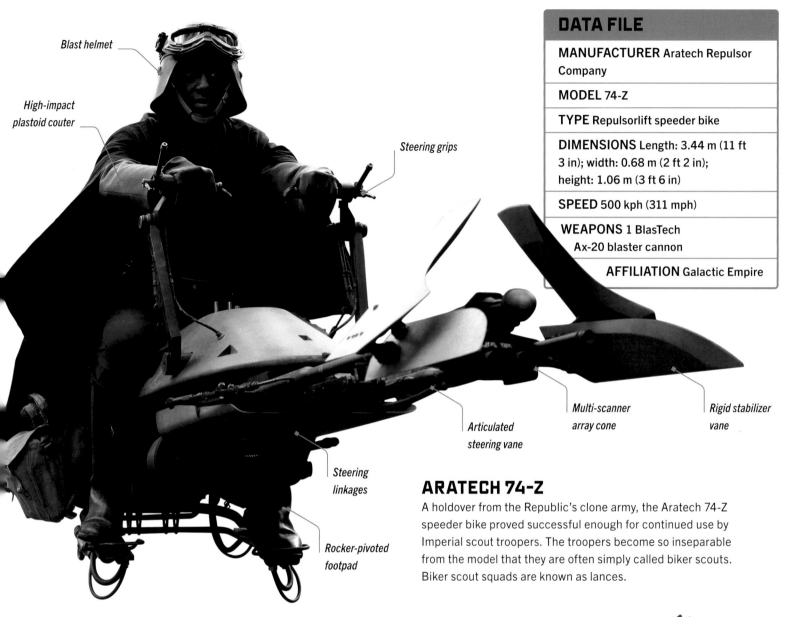

Blast helmet

High-impact
plastoid couter

Steering grips

Steering
linkages

Rocker-pivoted
footpad

Articulated
steering vane

Multi-scanner
array cone

Rigid stabilizer
vane

DATA FILE

MANUFACTURER Aratech Repulsor
Company

MODEL 74-Z

TYPE Repulsorlift speeder bike

DIMENSIONS Length: 3.44 m (11 ft
3 in); width: 0.68 m (2 ft 2 in);
height: 1.06 m (3 ft 6 in)

SPEED 500 kph (311 mph)

WEAPONS 1 BlasTech
Ax-20 blaster cannon

AFFILIATION Galactic Empire

ARATECH 74-Z

A holdover from the Republic's clone army, the Aratech 74-Z
speeder bike proved successful enough for continued use by
Imperial scout troopers. The troopers become so inseparable
from the model that they are often simply called biker scouts.
Biker scout squads are known as lances.

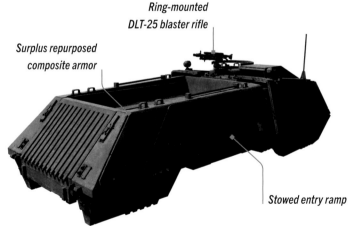

Ring-mounted
DLT-25 blaster rifle

Surplus repurposed
composite armor

Stowed entry ramp

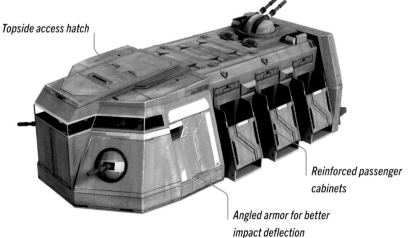

Topside access hatch

Reinforced passenger
cabinets

Angled armor for better
impact deflection

CSL-430 HOVER TRANSPORT

A simple armored skiff used for cargo or personnel transport, the CSL-430
is the result of reinforcing a civilian utility vehicle for military usage. It is
phased out as its more armored ITT successor is rolled out.

ITT

A dedicated armored personnel transport, the K79-S80 ITT also features passenger
restraints that make it an effective conveyance for shuttling prisoners overland.
The ITT's boxy design inspires the combat-oriented Trexler 906 Armored Marauder.

IMPERIAL EQUIPMENT

The Empire benefits from the biggest contractors developing gear for its fighting forces. Imperial equipment is well maintained, plentiful, and regularly reviewed for improvements. Manufacturers often compile reports on military equipment usage under the harshest of conditions, and then implement improvements into future editions of the kit or civilian incarnations of the gear.

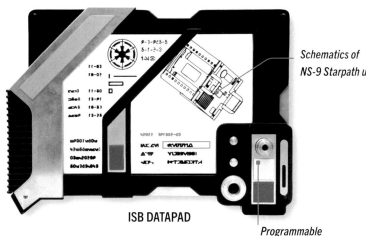

Schematics of
NS-9 Starpath unit

ISB DATAPAD

Programmable
user interface

Plastoid face mask frame

Filter cartridge
with vo-pickup
pass-through
amplifier

Corrugated
transfer hose

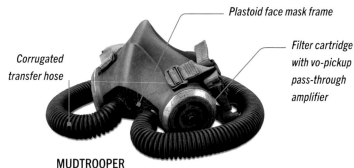

**MUDTROOPER
RESPIRATOR MASK**

Incandescent
storage level/
usage indicator

Vo-pickup
with noise
cancellation
filters

Hinged disc
access slot (stowed)

**DATA DISC
CARRIER**

**EMIGRATION
OFFICER COMMS**

Vo-pickup
microphone grill

Power cell recharge port

Viewing
shroud visor

**NEURO-SAAV MODEL TD2.3
ELECTROBINOCULARS**

Rubberized grip

C-1 COMLINK

Directional screen filter
ensures privacy

Water-sealed cooling vanes
with integral sand filters

Conductive plating for
neuro-shock charge

IMPERIAL BINDERS

**SHORETROOPER
E-11P BLASTER**

Tamper-resistant
chromium alloy casing

CODE CYLINDER

Scomp link
access ports

IMPERIAL CLERK DATAPAD

Electronic tamper detection indicator

CHAIN CODE BRIEFCASE

Stowed chain code identification cards

Hinged power cell casing

Servo-talus articulation joint

RANGE TROOPER MAGNATOMIC GRIPTION BOOTS

Imperial cogwheel sigil

Conductive contact tips

Exhaust filter channeling

STORMTROOPER RIOT CONTROL ELECTRO-PROD

Gas converter enabler chamber

Vocoder direct speaker grill

AT-ACT PILOT HELMET

Cooling fins

E-11 STORMTROOPER BLASTER

Outer lenses collect data from above and below visible spectrum

QD4.4 STORMTROOPER ELECTROQUADNOCULARS

Twist-activated time-delay trigger

DEATH TROOPER C-25 FRAGMENTATION GRENADE

Visibility slot

RIOT SHIELD

Power-setting dial

Carbonite-weave duroplast surface

Airtight seal

Inertial buffer field conductor rods

Captured kyber totem from Jedha shrine

KYBER CRYSTAL CONTAINER

Vaporator collection flask, seal, and cup

Vaporator condenser chiller bar

Grenade-carrying safety bracket

STORMTROOPER BACKPACK

CHAPTER 6

TOOLS OF THE REBELLION

The Rebellion makes the most of the gear on hand in its fight against the Empire. Battered weapons, vehicles, and equipment are used until they fall apart, and then cobbled together for use once again. However, the wide variations of equipment across the scattered rebel cells pose a challenge to Imperial tacticians, who must adapt to these unconventional and improvised assets.

REBEL SHIPS

The upper echelons of Imperial admiralty apply the word "fleet" to rebel ships with disdain, as the cobbled assembly of capital combat and support craft seem hardly a threat to the storied navy of the Galactic Empire. Sympathetic systems with capable defense forces have donated what they can to the fledgling Rebellion, and rebel commanders keep the fleet ever mobile to avoid Imperial detection, rarely massing together in significant numbers.

Elongated tail holds hyperdrive systems

Enlarged transparisteel viewport common to civilian ships

BREON DAYVAN
Antiquated and overproduced, Breon Dayvans have the advantage of anonymity as well as transponder systems that fail to trigger Imperial traffic control systems, making them ideal for undercover work.

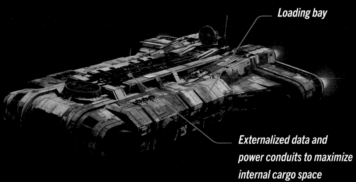

Loading bay

Externalized data and power conduits to maximize internal cargo space

JT-731 BROADHORN TRANSPORT
Refuse and maintenance carrier craft rarely get a second look from Imperial patrols, as their holds are rated for the transport of garbage. Early rebels refit them as secret refugee ships.

Dorsal landing pad

Articulated wing (open position)

Upgraded armor

PELTA-CLASS FRIGATE
A medical frigate design dating back to the waning days of the High Republic, the reliable *Pelta*-class still sees civilian usage. The rebels have turned the frigates into swift command ships.

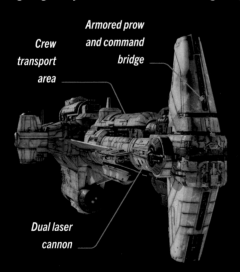

Crew transport area

Armored prow and command bridge

Dual laser cannon

SPHYRNA-CLASS CORVETTE
More commonly known as the Hammerhead corvette due to its distinct prow design, the Corellian made *Sphyrna*-class updates a classic design from the days of the Old Republic.

Primary deflector shield generator

Armored bow command module

BRAHA'TOK-CLASS GUNSHIP
The Dornean treaty with the Rebel Alliance brought their system patrol gunships into the fleet. Each *Braha'tok*-class gunship is armed with eight turbolaser cannons and missile launchers.

11-thruster ion turbine engine block

Principal reactor housing

Sensor pallet

CORELLIAN CORVETTE
The CR90 corvette has long served in local Corellian and Alderaanian fleets. The performance and ubiquity of these ships has made them famous as blockade runners.

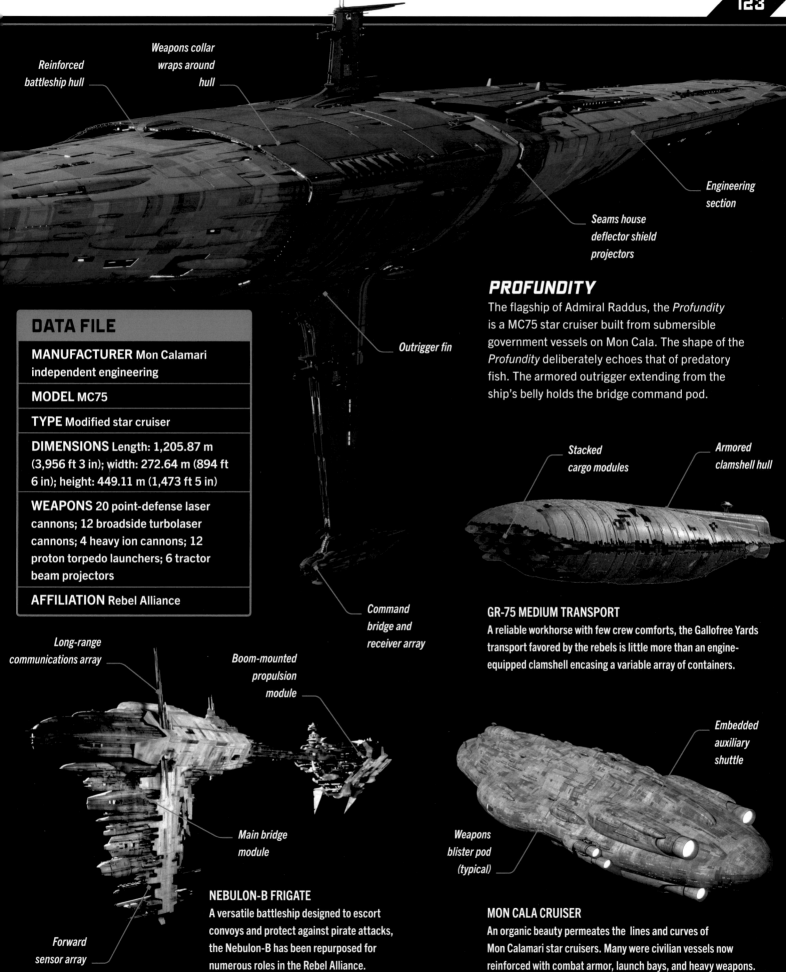

Reinforced battleship hull

Weapons collar wraps around hull

Engineering section

Seams house deflector shield projectors

Outrigger fin

Command bridge and receiver array

DATA FILE

MANUFACTURER Mon Calamari independent engineering

MODEL MC75

TYPE Modified star cruiser

DIMENSIONS Length: 1,205.87 m (3,956 ft 3 in); width: 272.64 m (894 ft 6 in); height: 449.11 m (1,473 ft 5 in)

WEAPONS 20 point-defense laser cannons; 12 broadside turbolaser cannons; 4 heavy ion cannons; 12 proton torpedo launchers; 6 tractor beam projectors

AFFILIATION Rebel Alliance

PROFUNDITY

The flagship of Admiral Raddus, the *Profundity* is a MC75 star cruiser built from submersible government vessels on Mon Cala. The shape of the *Profundity* deliberately echoes that of predatory fish. The armored outrigger extending from the ship's belly holds the bridge command pod.

Stacked cargo modules

Armored clamshell hull

GR-75 MEDIUM TRANSPORT

A reliable workhorse with few crew comforts, the Gallofree Yards transport favored by the rebels is little more than an engine-equipped clamshell encasing a variable array of containers.

Long-range communications array

Boom-mounted propulsion module

Main bridge module

Forward sensor array

NEBULON-B FRIGATE

A versatile battleship designed to escort convoys and protect against pirate attacks, the Nebulon-B has been repurposed for numerous roles in the Rebel Alliance.

Embedded auxiliary shuttle

Weapons blister pod (typical)

MON CALA CRUISER

An organic beauty permeates the lines and curves of Mon Calamari star cruisers. Many were civilian vessels now reinforced with combat armor, launch bays, and heavy weapons.

REBEL STARFIGHTERS

Starfighters are the single most valuable resource in the Rebel Alliance arsenal, according to military tacticians. Advanced, cutting-edge designs are difficult to procure, so the rebel inventory includes captured prototypes, vintage models, and experimental designs whose development was kept secret by loyal engineers and senatorial supervisors. The result is a varied mix of potent craft.

X-WING FIGHTER

The most famous of Rebel Alliance craft, the Incom T-65 X-wing starfighter emphasizes the pilot as its most important component, with shields, hyperdrive, and weapon systems maximized for the protection of its crew. The effectiveness of X-wing strikes has increasingly worried Imperial commanders and strategists.

T-47 AIRSPEEDER

The airspeeder's repulsorlifts require gravitational mass to push against, which prevents the T-47 from being a starfighter. However, its similar controls make it a useful pilot training craft and, in dire need, an option for engagements in planetary atmospheres.

Salvaged armor hull plating

Power converter for laser cannon

Expanded cabin holds two passengers and a pilot

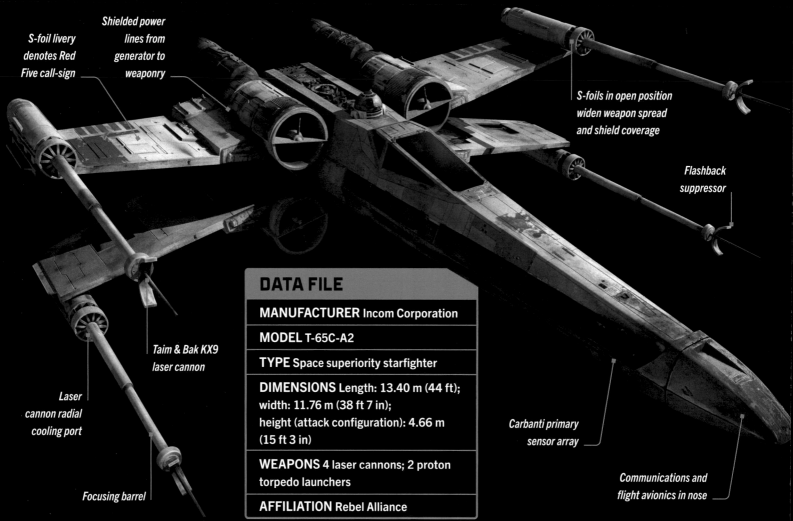

S-foil livery denotes Red Five call-sign

Shielded power lines from generator to weaponry

S-foils in open position widen weapon spread and shield coverage

Flashback suppressor

Taim & Bak KX9 laser cannon

Laser cannon radial cooling port

Carbanti primary sensor array

Focusing barrel

Communications and flight avionics in nose

DATA FILE

MANUFACTURER Incom Corporation	
MODEL T-65C-A2	
TYPE Space superiority starfighter	
DIMENSIONS Length: 13.40 m (44 ft); width: 11.76 m (38 ft 7 in); height (attack configuration): 4.66 m (15 ft 3 in)	
WEAPONS 4 laser cannons; 2 proton torpedo launchers	
AFFILIATION Rebel Alliance	

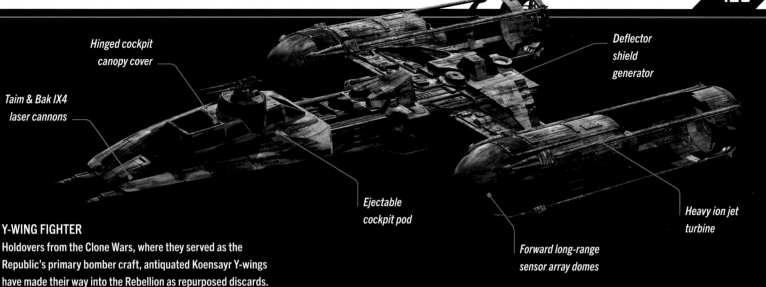

Hinged cockpit canopy cover

Deflector shield generator

Taim & Bak IX4 laser cannons

Ejectable cockpit pod

Heavy ion jet turbine

Forward long-range sensor array domes

Y-WING FIGHTER

Holdovers from the Clone Wars, where they served as the Republic's primary bomber craft, antiquated Koensayr Y-wings have made their way into the Rebellion as repurposed discards.

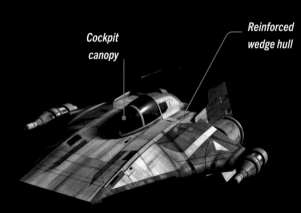

Cockpit canopy

Reinforced wedge hull

A-WING FIGHTER

A swift interceptor used effectively in the Lothal sector by the Phoenix cell, the KSE RZ-1 A-wing is a heavily modified craft originally rejected by the Empire.

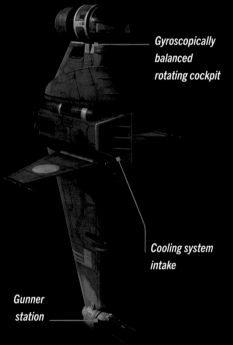

Gyroscopically balanced rotating cockpit

Cooling system intake

Gunner station

BLADE WING

A prototype heavy starfighter developed by a Mon Calamari engineer named Quarrie, the Blade Wing is a complex attack craft with a weapons loadout capable of challenging capital ships.

Rotating cockpit collar

Retro thruster nozzles

B-WING

The success of Quarrie's prototype was turned by the Verpine shipbuilders of the Slayn and Korpil hives into the A/SF-01 B-wing starfighter, a powerful attack ship loaded with weaponry.

Energy intake cooling vanes

Incom 4J.7 fusial thrust engine

Articulated S-foils in stowed position

U-WING STARFIGHTER/TRANSPORT

A versatile gunship and troop transport produced in relatively small numbers, the U-wing is one of the last designs from Incom before the company's nationalization by the Empire.

> "WE HAVE BEEN REDIRECTED TO SCARIF. PILOTS, YOU'LL BE BRIEFED BY YOUR SQUADRON LEADERS EN ROUTE. MAY THE FORCE BE WITH YOU."
>
> – WEDGE ANTILLES

REBEL SPEEDER BIKES

Whereas the Empire has many military contractors eager to equip the expanding war machine, the resource-strapped Rebel Alliance must look elsewhere for vehicles to fill their repulsorpools. Repurposed civilian craft form the bulk of rebel speeder designs, with custom designs being the norm rather than the exception. The gamut runs from speeders lovingly tended as an extension of the owner, to simple and expedient tools meant to be discarded at a moment's notice when a mission requires.

DATA FILE

MANUFACTURER	Ikas-Adno
MODEL	NovaKite 35-E Porto
TYPE	Speeder bike
DIMENSIONS	Length: 2.42 m (7 ft 11 in); width: 0.72 m (2 ft 4 in); height: 1.09 m (3 ft 7 in)
SPEED	450 kph (280 mph)
WEAPONS	None
AFFILIATION	Civilian

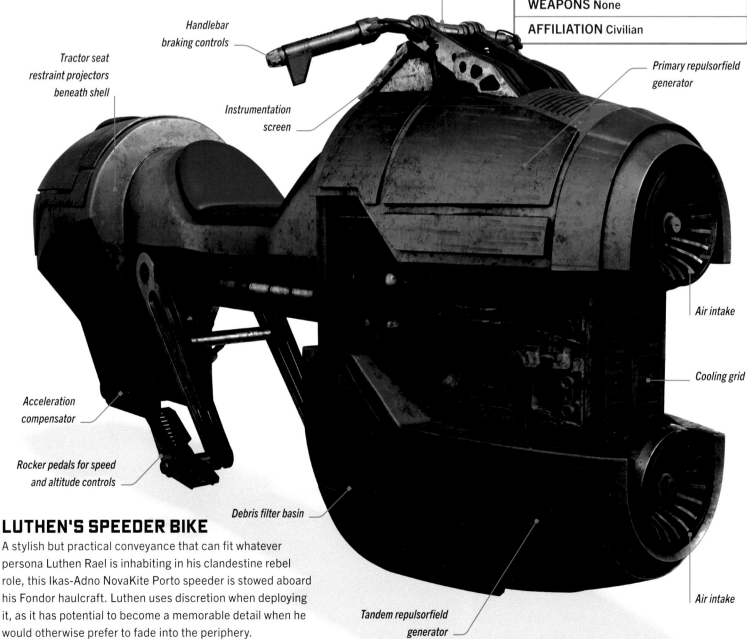

Articulated handlebar

Handlebar braking controls

Instrumentation screen

Tractor seat restraint projectors beneath shell

Primary repulsorfield generator

Air intake

Cooling grid

Acceleration compensator

Rocker pedals for speed and altitude controls

Debris filter basin

Tandem repulsorfield generator

Air intake

LUTHEN'S SPEEDER BIKE

A stylish but practical conveyance that can fit whatever persona Luthen Rael is inhabiting in his clandestine rebel role, this Ikas-Adno NovaKite Porto speeder is stowed aboard his Fondor haulcraft. Luthen uses discretion when deploying it, as it has potential to become a memorable detail when he would otherwise prefer to fade into the periphery.

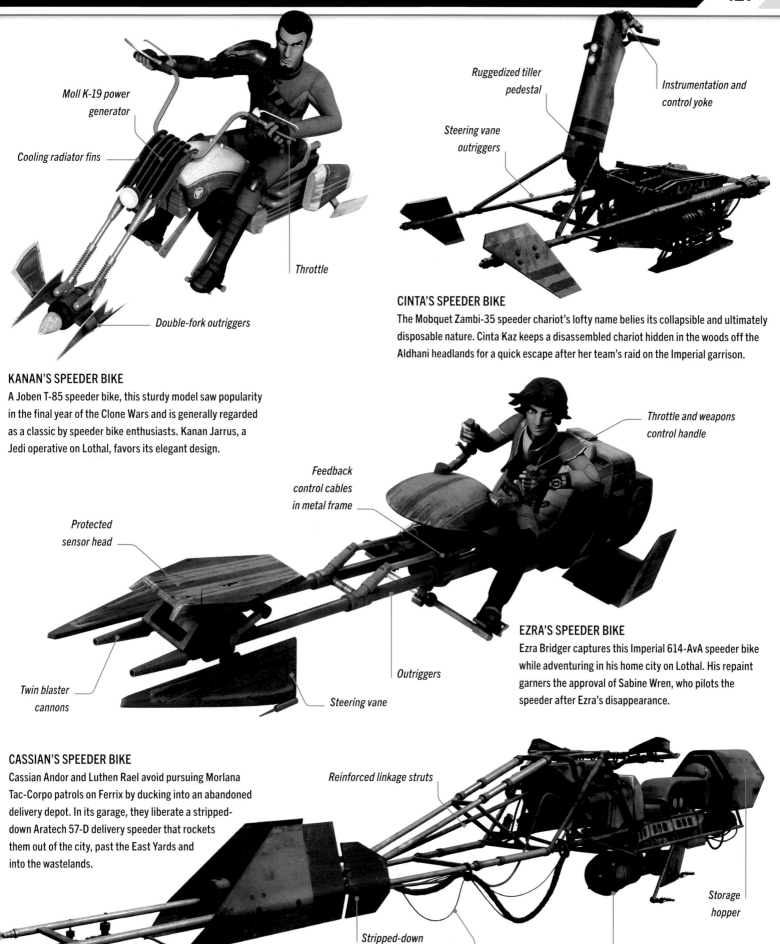

Moll K-19 power
generator

Cooling radiator fins

Throttle

Double-fork outriggers

KANAN'S SPEEDER BIKE
A Joben T-85 speeder bike, this sturdy model saw popularity in the final year of the Clone Wars and is generally regarded as a classic by speeder bike enthusiasts. Kanan Jarrus, a Jedi operative on Lothal, favors its elegant design.

Ruggedized tiller
pedestal

Steering vane
outriggers

Instrumentation and
control yoke

CINTA'S SPEEDER BIKE
The Mobquet Zambi-35 speeder chariot's lofty name belies its collapsible and ultimately disposable nature. Cinta Kaz keeps a disassembled chariot hidden in the woods off the Aldhani headlands for a quick escape after her team's raid on the Imperial garrison.

Throttle and weapons
control handle

Feedback
control cables
in metal frame

Protected
sensor head

Twin blaster
cannons

Outriggers

Steering vane

EZRA'S SPEEDER BIKE
Ezra Bridger captures this Imperial 614-AvA speeder bike while adventuring in his home city on Lothal. His repaint garners the approval of Sabine Wren, who pilots the speeder after Ezra's disappearance.

CASSIAN'S SPEEDER BIKE
Cassian Andor and Luthen Rael avoid pursuing Morlana Tac-Corpo patrols on Ferrix by ducking into an abandoned delivery depot. In its garage, they liberate a stripped-down Aratech 57-D delivery speeder that rockets them out of the city, past the East Yards and into the wastelands.

Reinforced linkage struts

Storage
hopper

Stripped-down
modified steering vanes

Exposed control cables

Aratech repulsorlift generator

REBEL EQUIPMENT

Rebel equipment often tends to be improvised, modified, and used until it falls apart. The Alliance must make do with the gear on hand, but as the Rebellion matures, so, too, does its supply chain. Sympathetic manufacturers, politicians, and traders have found ways to strategically "misplace" shipments or have them deliberately targeted by rebel raiders so they remain innocent. The care put into the upkeep of rebel hardware often makes it the equal of more expensive Imperial counterparts.

Stellar goniophotometer

KARIS NEMIK'S ASTRONAVE UNIT

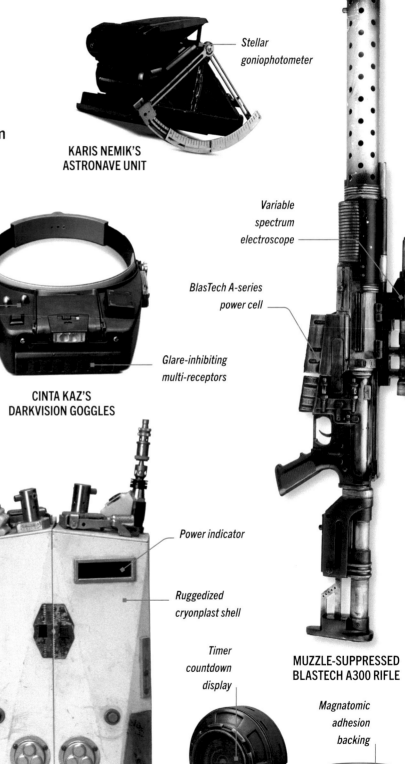

Variable spectrum electroscope

BlasTech A-series power cell

MUZZLE-SUPPRESSED BLASTECH A300 RIFLE

Passive-scan EM lenses

NEURO-SAAV TE1.3 QUADNOCULARS

Image enhancement processors

Glare-inhibiting multi-receptors

CINTA KAZ'S DARKVISION GOGGLES

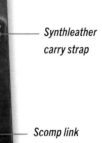

Synthleather carry strap

Scomp link access ports

CAPTAIN CASSIAN ANDOR'S INTELLIGENCE DATAPAD

Retracted motorized antenna

Power indicator

Ruggedized cryonplast shell

Timer countdown display

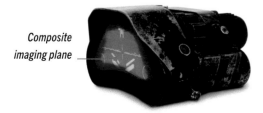

Composite imaging plane

FABRITECH Q4-E QUADNOCULARS

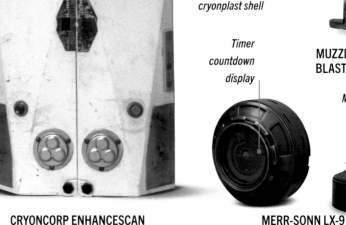

CRYONCORP ENHANCESCAN PORTABLE SCANNER

Magnatomic adhesion backing

MERR-SONN LX-9 SLAP CHARGES

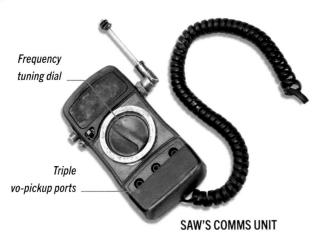

Frequency tuning dial

Triple vo-pickup ports

SAW'S COMMS UNIT

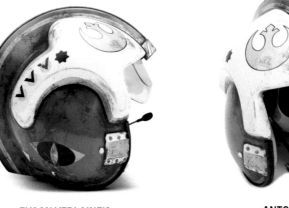

EVAAN VERLAINE'S HELMET (GOLD THREE)

ANTOC MERRICK'S HELMET (BLUE LEADER)

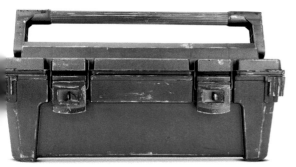

CASSIAN ANDOR'S U-WING TOOLBOX

WADE RESSELIAN'S HELMET

ZAL DINNES' HELMET (RED EIGHT)

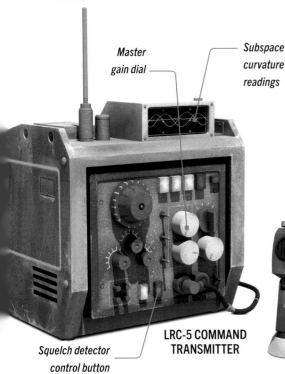

Master gain dial

Subspace curvature readings

Magnetically affixed spare blaster gas cartridge

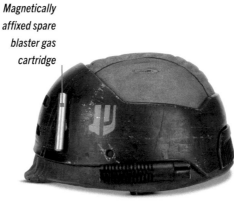

Hand-held vo-pickup

Squelch detector control button

LRC-5 COMMAND TRANSMITTER

PATHFINDER HELMET

Fragmenting outer shell

KF-2 GRENADE

Trigger calibrated to Roken's strength

KAWLAN ROKEN'S ZP08 BLASTER PISTOL

Carry ring fastener

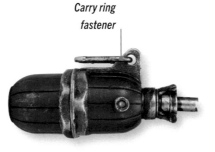

C-35 FRAGMENTATION GRENADE

SULLY STARK'S HELMET

CHAPTER 7

PRELUDE TO WAR

Hidden in orbit over Scarif, the Death Star nears completion as part of the Emperor's unthinkable endgame. With the power to threaten planetary destruction at his whim, the Emperor plans to quell any rebellion through the fear the battle station provokes. Ironically, the Death Star's existence only galvanizes the fledgling Rebellion into action. At Scarif, the first shots of the Galactic Civil War are fired.

YAVIN 4

After abandoning rebel outposts on Dantooine, Garel, and Atollon, the cells based on those planets and others gather at Yavin 4. The system is but a footnote in Imperial cartography, as its gaseous principal planet is not economically viable or strategically desirable. Neither do its collection of moons warrant cataloging, despite three of them being capable of supporting humanoid life. Thanks to its obscurity and accessibility, Yavin 4 is a prize discovery for the Rebellion.

VITAL SENTRIES

The electromagnetic noise produced by the gas giant shields Yavin 4 from passive sensor scans, and could mask enemy ships on approach. Flesh-and-blood sentries stand atop observation towers as a last line of defense, ready to alert the base of any unexpected deviations in flightpaths.

THE GREAT TEMPLE

The ziggurat of the Great Temple is the largest of the ancient structures in what has been named the Massassi site to honor the long-vanished builders of the stone edifices. Rebel engineers have much to work with, as the well-built pyramid has withstood the ravages of time and weather for millennia. They have carefully threaded power and utility conduits through the five terraces, building in turbolift clusters to provide easier level-to-level transit than the ancient staircases that line the vine-covered exterior.

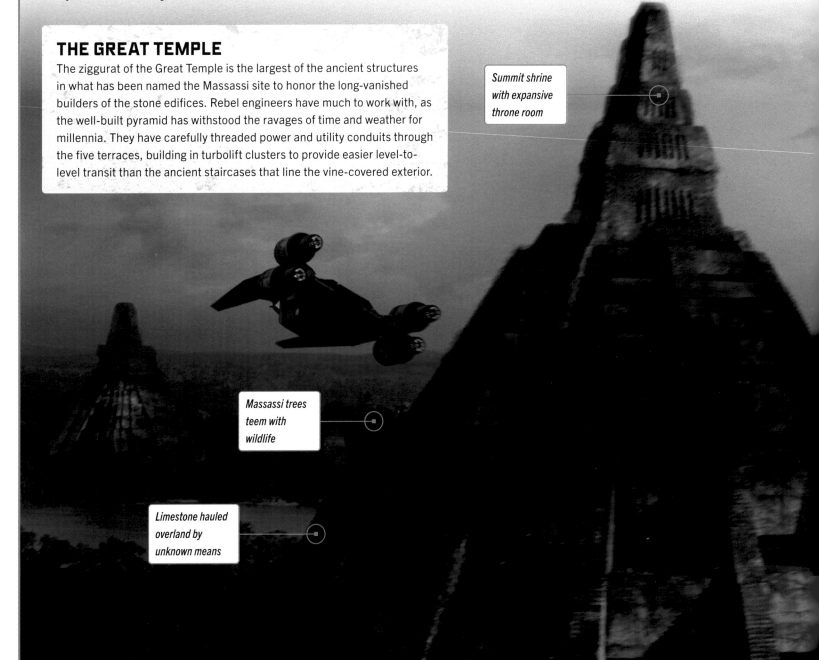

Summit shrine with expansive throne room

Massassi trees teem with wildlife

Limestone hauled overland by unknown means

COMMAND CENTER

Located within the third terrace of the massive ziggurat is the command center of the Massassi Base. Summit-mounted sensors and communications equipment collect information from discreet orbital relays. These pierce the ever-present electromagnetic haze from the gas giant, keeping the Base One command center connected to its patrol ships. A large holographic display table forms the centerpiece of the room. Tacticians monitor communications and sensor signatures, manually updating positional data on tracking screens to create an abstract yet real-time view of rapidly changing conditions.

HANGAR

Base One's entire ground level has been repurposed into a hangar and launch bay. Modern refueling ports and power supply lines snake through the ancient alcoves. Pilots navigate the enclosure with precision repulsorlift maneuvering, coordinated by ground crew marshals.

LANDING ZONE

The ground floor is primarily dedicated to housing starfighters, leaving the cleared grounds before the temple as an exterior landing strip for larger vessels. Antiquated ships or those experiencing damage may need an obstruction-free expanse for safe landings. Technicians bring in portable power and victualing tanks as needed.

Exterior staging area abuts the Temple of the Blueleaf Cluster

Cries of arboreal howler lizards carry for miles

YAVIN 4 PERSONNEL

Aggregated from several splintered units into a command structure, the leadership of the Massassi Base is far more orderly than was typical of the rebellion just a few years earlier. The outpost's personnel are organized according to a historic Alderaanian military model, with traditional ranks and service divisions delineating a flow of operations. By necessity, though, the rebels must be flexible to adapt to their unpredictable circumstances. At a moment's notice, the entire unit can be evacuated to avoid Imperial reprisal.

GENERAL DRAVEN

Alliance Intelligence chief Davits Draven is a pragmatic, calculating officer often tasked with making difficult decisions while lives hang in the balance. He does not underestimate the Empire's cruelty.

GENERAL MERRICK

An experienced starfighter pilot from Virujansi, General Antoc Merrick oversees starfighter operations on Yavin 4. He flies Blue One, the lead X-wing fighter of Blue Squadron.

COMMANDER WILLARD

Vanden Huyck Willard is a sector commander from Sulorine who transfers to Yavin 4 to offer his expertise. He is quite close to the Alderaanian delegation, having offered intelligence services to Bail and Leia Organa in the past.

ADMIRAL RADDUS

The fleet commander for the Alliance's growing naval forces, Admiral Raddus was a civilian defense leader on Mon Cala until the Imperial occupation of his homeworld forced him to join the rebellion. His flagship, *Profundity*, is one of the first Mon Calamari combat vessels in the rebel fleet.

COMMANDER HUDSOL

Bob Hudsol is a sector commander from Corellia who prioritizes transfer to Alliance High Command as the conflict with the Empire escalates. A military history scholar, Hudsol is a skilled starfighter combat tactician.

Raddus is a stern, direct leader. Focused on strategy, he leaves the political viewpoints to others.

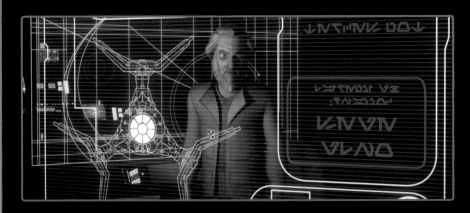

While aiding Phoenix cell Dodonna focuses on starfighter strategy, particularly in countering the new threats like the TIE defender prototype. Dodonna believes future victory to be dependent on fighter combat superiority.

GENERAL DODONNA

A senior officer and lead strategist aboard the frigate *Vanguard*, Jan Dodonna brings with him a lifetime of military experience. He was a bridge officer aboard the *Venator*-class Star Destroyer *Guardian* during the Clone Wars, and continues his naval career in the emergent Empire before coming to appreciate the true nature of the Imperial war machine. A dramatic defection secretly facilitated by Bail Organa brings him into the growing Rebellion.

The advancing age of certain command staff has earned them the nickname the Gray Cadre.

DATA FILE

SUBJECT	Jan Dodonna
HOMEWORLD	Commenor
SPECIES	Human
AFFILIATION	Rebel Alliance
HEIGHT	1.82 m (6 ft)
AGE	64 (1 BBY)

Service uniforms of classic Alderaanian design

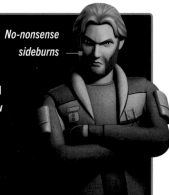

CAPTAIN KALLUS

No-nonsense sideburns

A former agent of the Imperial Security Bureau, Alexsandr Kallus defected to the rebel cause. He now provides vital intel and insight on Imperial operations directly to Alliance High Command.

LIEUTENANT VERLAINE

Evaan Verlaine flies as Gold Three as part of Dutch Vander's Gold Squadron. She was born and raised on Alderaan and is a staunch royalist, having been mentored by Queen Breha Organa.

DROID UNITS

Operational security means that these support droids from the *Tantive IV*, like all personnel without a need to know, are unaware of the location of Yavin 4 even when on its surface.

TranLang III communications module

Multi-spectrum central photoreceptor

DEATH STAR CONSTRUCTION

A project as immense as the Death Star requires construction at sites spread across the galaxy, with components joined together at the final assembly site in orbit over Scarif. The earliest phases of construction began over Geonosis, where automated factories and Geonosian drones labored to build the skeletal framework for the colossal craft. Individual components were developed in secret at shipyards loyal to the Imperial military. Security concerns led to the relocation of the gestating Death Star to Scarif, after enough bureaucratic subterfuge created the plausible cover story of an energy-generating initiative spearheaded by the Emperor.

NARKINA 5

A habitable moon in orbit of the gas giant Narkina, Narkina 5 is a watery world of massive lakes. Formerly an industrial quarry, it has been completely isolated by the Empire to serve as a prison. The water-bound Imperial prison is seven levels of unrelenting drudgery and grueling quotas.

The manager of factory floor 5-2-D, Kino Loy runs his room with methodical efficiency, maximizing the output of 49 men.

Electromagnetic-reactive transluciplast coating

Tamper indicator displays time of last access

Carry handle

Monomolecular-switching binary tape protected by laminate seal

DEATH STAR PLANS

The shifting schedules and evolving details of the Death Star project require the constant updating of schematics. The complete archives of the project code-named Stardust are secured in the data vault at the Imperial Citadel on Scarif. A high-density data cartridge is kept isolated and disconnected from any network interface for security purposes—contact with the plans must be made physically.

The data cartridge resides inside a hermetically sealed data-tree assembly within the Structural Node of the Scarif vault. Servo-manipulators allow archivists to remove the tapes for reference and inspection.

Access to the vault is constrained to sensor-lined corridors that also include powerful degausser-field emitters to remotely erase any datatapes within them should a breach be detected.

The Citadel is a well-armed and armored command base in the atolls of Scarif primarily tasked with monitoring construction and weapon test projects. Scarif itself is protected by a powerful energy shield.

ASSEMBLY LINE

DECENTRALIZED CONSTRUCTION
Each Narkina 5 workroom has seven tables with seven men quickly assembling components to reach quotas for meager rewards.

FINISHED PARTS
The identical completed components are automatically moved down to storage while the parts for the next one replace them.

DROID ASSEMBLY
Worker droids place the components into sockets in the orbital construction zone high above Scarif, locking them into alignment.

THE SUPERLASER
The components are simple panel joins that keep receptor cells in alignment within the focusing lens of the Death Star superlaser.

Firing field amplifier

Outer focusing lens shapes the kyber amplifier field

Secondary lensing body with eight subsidiary stream ports

Core reactor tap and power diverter

COMING TOGETHER

From the core reactor tap at the base of the superlaser to the focusing eye at its surface terminus, this weapon is the most labor-intensive subassembly of the Death Star, requiring several from-scratch redesigns in its overlong construction history. It finally nears perfection over Scarif.

TIMELINE

22 BBY	The initial plans secretly delivered to Chancellor Palpatine
20 BBY	Clandestine construction of the Death Star begins
18 BBY	Phase Three of construction focuses on hyperreactor and shield generator work
17 BBY	Galen Erso flees the project in a fit of conscience
13 BBY	Director Krennic brings Galen to Eadu to focus on kyber crystal research
9 BBY	Construction of the Death Star relocated from Geonosis to Scarif
5 BBY	Materials breakthrough revamps latest iteration of superlaser
1 BBY	Single reactor ignition test of superlaser at Jedha

DEATH STAR LEADERSHIP

It is to be the ultimate tool of authority and control, assembled in secret far from the prying eyes of the Senate: the Death Star battle station. With the threat of planetary annihilation, the Emperor can do away with the formal tools of governance and rule the galaxy by fear. Such an ambitious project takes decades to deliver, as supply shortages and technical setbacks plague its cutting-edge development. The Emperor's need for secrecy further hampers the likelihood of a timely construction of a workable weapon.

It falls to a secret cabal of military leaders and engineering geniuses to bring this destructive vision to reality. As the Death Star holds such personal interest to Palpatine, it creates an undercurrent of competition among the leadership personnel and more than a little infighting.

DIRECTOR KRENNIC

With time and the Emperor's patience fast running out, Orson Krennic walks a razor's edge. He needs to finalize the Death Star but without too much assistance—which would diminish his own prestige upon success. He is particularly wary of Governor Tarkin, who he sees as ready to swoop in to claim credit or cast blame depending on how the fortunes of Project Stardust fall.

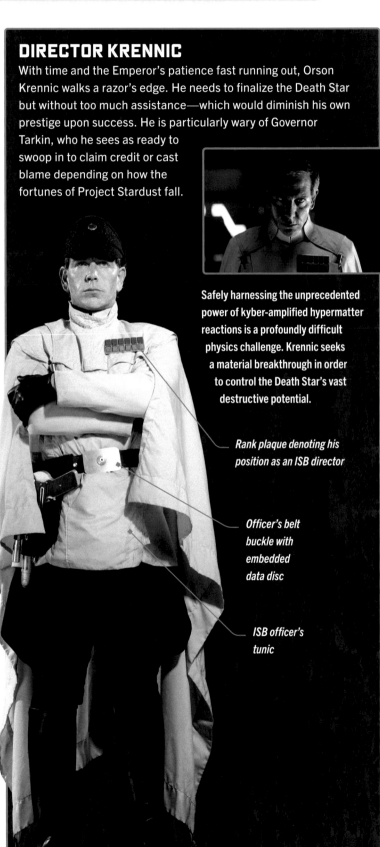

Safely harnessing the unprecedented power of kyber-amplified hypermatter reactions is a profoundly difficult physics challenge. Krennic seeks a material breakthrough in order to control the Death Star's vast destructive potential.

Rank plaque denoting his position as an ISB director

Officer's belt buckle with embedded data disc

ISB officer's tunic

ADMIRAL MOTTI

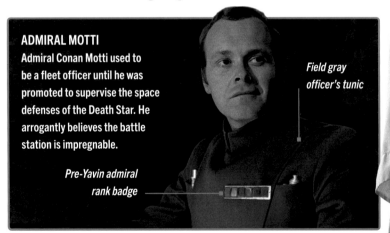

Admiral Conan Motti used to be a fleet officer until he was promoted to supervise the space defenses of the Death Star. He arrogantly believes the battle station is impregnable.

Field gray officer's tunic

Pre-Yavin admiral rank badge

GENERAL ROMODI

Hurst Romodi is a Clone Wars veteran who saw firsthand the destruction a chaotic galaxy can yield. He has supervised the distribution of the Imperial military across numerous trouble-filled sectors and helped quash dissent in the unruly Western Reaches.

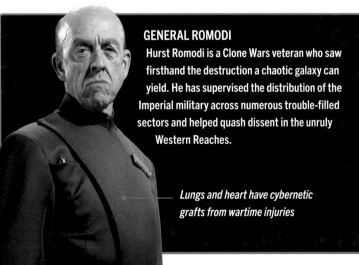

Lungs and heart have cybernetic grafts from wartime injuries

GENERAL TAGGE

An unimaginative if competent army officer, General Cassio Tagge's political influence stems from his well-heeled family of nobles, collectively the House of Tagge. He is one of the few in the upper ranks to voice misgivings about the Death Star's effectiveness against the growing rebel threat.

> **"THIS STATION IS NOW THE ULTIMATE POWER IN THE UNIVERSE. I SUGGEST WE USE IT."**
> – ADMIRAL CONAN MOTTI

GALEN ERSO

A gifted polymath who applies his intellectual brilliance to energy research, Galen Erso makes significant breakthroughs in kyber crystal experimentation. Inspired by the Jedi, who have long used kyber as a focusing crystal in their lightsabers, Erso naively envisions a future where abundant energy will solve many of the galaxy's problems. Such naivety is exploited by his friend Orson Krennic.

Rank cylinder with clearance codes

Science and Engineering Division rank plaque

Realizing with horror what his knowledge is being used for, Galen flees the Empire with his wife Lyra and his daughter Jyn to live in exile on a homestead on Lah'mu.

> **"WE CALL IT THE DEATH STAR. THERE IS NO BETTER NAME... AND THE DAY IS COMING SOON WHEN IT WILL BE UNLEASHED."**
> – GALEN ERSO

"IT IS A PERIOD OF
CIVIL WAR...."

INDEX

TEEGA KRYELLE

TIME
GRAPPLER

EDRIO
TWO-TUBES

TIE FIGHTER

Penguin
Random
House

Senior Editor Matt Jones
Editor Frankie Hallam
Project Art Editor Chris Gould
Production Editor Siu Yin Chan
Senior Production Controller Mary Slater
Managing Editor Emma Grange
Managing Art Editor Vicky Short
Publishing Director Mark Searle

Designed for DK by Ray Bryant, Simon Murrell, and Colin Williams

FOR LUCASFILM
Senior Editor Brett Rector
Creative Director of Publishing Michael Siglain
Art Director Troy Alders
Concept Artists Jon McCoy, David Dobbins, Thang Le,
Ralph McQuarrie, Erik Tiemens, and Andrée Wallin
Asset Management Chris Argyropoulos, Gabrielle Levenson,
Micaela McCauley, Elinor De La Torre, Bryce Pinkos,
Michael Trobiani, and Sarah Williams
Story Group Leland Chee, Kate Izquierdo,
Matt Martin, and Phil Szostak

First published in Great Britain in 2023 by
Dorling Kindersley Limited
DK, One Embassy Gardens, 8 Viaduct Gardens,
London, SW11 7BW

The authorised representative in the EEA is
Dorling Kindersley Verlag GmbH. Arnulfstr. 124,
80636 Munich, Germany

ACKNOWLEDGMENTS

Pablo Hidalgo: Thanks to the live-action production teams that have been so inviting in welcoming me into their amazing worlds as they are built. It was a pleasure chatting lore with Deborah Chow, Joby Harold, Tony Gilroy, David Girvan, Sanne Wohlenberg, and all the artists on their shows. Thanks to my colleagues at the Lucasfilm Story Group for their deft skills in helping spin so many plates. Thanks to ILM's Ryan A. Smith for measuring digital ship models down to the centimeter. Much appreciation to Emily for their collaboration on this project. And special thanks to Barry Gingell for tracking down a candid photo of the ever-elusive Anto Kreegyr.

Emily Shkoukani: To Pablo Hidalgo, you wrote most of this book but the pages you didn't are dedicated to you. Thank you for advocating for me and sharing a love for *Revenge of the Sith*. To DK, whose books have always taken up shelves in my home, thank you for welcoming me into the family and trusting me. Thank you to the Lucasfilm Story Group and Publishing team for their support. Thank you to my family for always quizzing me on *Star Wars*. And thank you to Colin and my kitties for keeping me company while writing.

John R. Mullaney: I would like to thank Chris Gould, Matt Jones, Vicky Short, Sophie Dryburgh, Becky Watts, Clive Savage, and all the team at DK for their friendly collaboration & support; Pablo Hidalgo at Lucasfilm for his helpful notes and encyclopedic insight; and to my friend (and *Andor* Extra) Nicky Nustar Clark for his Luthen body-double vectors. Additional thanks to my family—ever my bedrock, to the inspirational Hans Jenssen and Richard Chasemore for setting the high benchmark, and to the filmmakers for creating an incredible series and coming up with the most gadget-packed ship in the galaxy.

DK Publishing: DK would like to thank Pablo Hidalgo, Emily Shkoukani, and John R. Mullaney for their contributions to the book; Megan Douglass for proofreading and Americanizing; Julia March for proofreading and indexing; and Chelsea Alon at Disney.

Medical supplement port

Multipurpose bandolier fitt with saboteu tools